"Dust In The Wind"

The Civil War In Indian Territory

By Ethel Crisp Taylor

Copyright © 2005
Ethel Crisp Taylor
55500 Bates Road Bandon OR 97411
ISBN: 0-7884-3276-1

All rights reserved. No part of this book may be reproduced or transmitted in any form or by any means, electronic or mechanical, including photocopying, recording or by any information storage and retrieval system without written permission by the author, except for brief quotations in a review.

This book is dedicated to those Nations' soldiers who fought in drastic conditions during 1861-1865. Mounted on their Indian ponies, they fought with little food, outdated weapons, scarce supplies and sparse clothing. Supplies were hard to come by, so they took what they came upon.

They lost everything in the war: homes, loved ones, livestock, crops. Yet they fought for what they believed. Whether they fought for Blue or Gray, they must be remembered.

We would be remiss, if we did not mention the Texas and Arkansas troops who fought alongside them.

May their descendents be proud of them, and remember their sacrifices!

Author's Notes

I began researching my families some years ago. I found I had fourteen Confederate ancestors and three Union. Being also of Cherokee descent and growing up in Oklahoma, I was interested in information about the Cherokee during this time period. Information was scarce on whatever part the Indians had during the War Between the States. So began my research into this era in Indian Territory. There were no answers to be easily found.

As I delved deeper into this research, I found few books on the subject, and those I did find, did not cover much information. I also discovered many of the people of the Nations involved had little knowledge of that period. Known names were John Ross, Principal Chief of the Cherokee at that time; General Stand Watie, the last field general to lay down his arms; and, perhaps lesser known, Eli Parker, a Seneca staff officer with General Grant. Some 20,000 Western and Eastern Indians were drawn into this conflict as soldiers or auxiliaries of the United States or the Confederate States.

Although there were actions in Arkansas and Missouri during this period, I kept to only the actions in Indian Territory, or those outside, where the Confederate Indians participated. The Union Indian Brigades were in some of the actions outside the Territory; again I mention only those where both sides participated.

This journey has taken me through those four years of strife. I hope to share some of the intrigue, actions, elation, heartbreak and pain of those years and the people who lived through them. Live with the Southern Indians, hear the Rebel yells, smell the dust and gun smoke of the battles, as you travel with these warriors through 1861-1865.

This is their story. It is my hope that these pages will be a monument for those forgotten soldiers in gray, so that their descendents will know what they did. Be proud of your ancestors, whether in gray or blue, for they fought for their beliefs. Don't let them be forgotten...

As Dust in The Wind!

CONTENTS

Title Page	
Copyright Page	
Dedication	iii
Author's Notes	iv
Acknowledgments	ix
Introduction	x
Chapter 1 1861	1
Governor Rector to Chief Ross	2
Pike's Letter	9
Wilson's Creek, MO	17
Chapter 2	21
O-Pothle-Yahola to Lincoln	22
Ross's Letter to McCulloch, Reply	23
Ross's Message to Cherokee Nation	25
Cherokee Declaration	29
Chapter 3	39
Round Mountain, IT	39
Chusto-Talasah/Bird Creek, IT	48
Chustenalah/Caving Banks/Shoal Creek, IT	57
Chapter 4 1862	63
Elk Horn Tavern/Pea Ridge, AR	70
Chapter 5	83
Neosho, MO	83
Cowskin Prairie, IT	86
Lt. Phillips' Message to Ross	88
Spavinaw Creek/Locust Grove, IT	90
Greeno's Speech to Cherokee	95
Pike's Resignation	102
Carthage, MO	105
Neutonia, MO	106
Fort Wayne, IT	108

Tonkawa Creek/Wichita Agency/ Fort Cobb, IT	109
Fort Davis, IT	115
Chapter 6 1863	117
Fort Gibson, IT	118
Watie's Address to Cherokee Council	119
First Cabin Creek, IT	124
Honey Springs, IT	130
Perryville, IT	135
Billie Bowleggs, et.al, to Agent Snow	137
Chapter 7 1864	143
General Maxey's Address to Grand Council of Five Nations	143
Middle Boggy, IT	145
Poison Springs, AR	148
Pleasant Bluff, IT	154
Massard Prairie, AR	160
Fort Smith, AR	161
Flat Rock, IT	163
Colonel Barker's Report	165
Second Cabin Creek, IT	166
General Gano's Report	170
Pryor Creek, IT	171
Telegram, Perry Fuller to Commissioner Dole, I. A.	172
Memo to President Lincoln from Lewis Downing	175
Chapter 8 1865	181
Snake Creek, IT	184
Cease Fire Treaty	185
Sale of Old Arkansas Cherokee Agency	190
1866 Treaty, USA – Cherokee Nation, Southern Cherokee	192
Important Sites in Indian Territory	198

Indian Territory Maps	215
Resources	219

Acknowledgments

The authors who came before helped to make this offering possible. Information was gathered from many sources. This effort is an attempt to pull all of it together. Deep gratitude goes to all whose efforts expanded on my search.

Much appreciation goes to my family, for their love, support and encouragement, during the difficult search times. And to my husband, who ever so patiently waited for me on many research trips and who accompanied me in visiting the battle sites we were able to locate in Oklahoma. It made for many hot, dusty summer days.

And of course, the ladies at the Bandon, OR Public Library and that marvelous nationwide library link, known as the Interlibrary Loan System! Thanks to them, they brought the research material to me, since I could not travel to the various libraries where I needed to go. Without their help, this could not have been accomplished. Thank you!

Ethel Crisp Taylor

INTRODUCTION

"The only allies of the Confederacy, the five Indian Nations of the Creek, Cherokees, Seminoles, Choctaws and Chickasaws in the War Between The States, suffered a larger percent of losses than did any of the other states"
Confederate Memorial Hall
Oklahoma Historical Society
Dedicated to "The Forgotten Heroes 1861-1865"

    The Indian Nations are considered Sovereign Nations, and as such, were the only sovereign foreign Nations to be allies of the Confederacy on the same continent.

    In 1861 the area of present-day Oklahoma was known as "Indian Territory". About 60,000 Choctaw, Cherokee, Chickasaw, Creek and Seminole Indians resided in the Territory with 1,500 white men married to Indian women, and 10,000 Negro slaves. An estimated 2,500 Osage, Caddo, Wichita, Shawnee, and Delaware were part of the I. T. population and approximately 3,000 Comanche, Kiowa, Cheyenne and Arapaho were located in the western part of Oklahoma, the Texas panhandle, southeast Colorado and southwest Kansas. Of these people, 8,000 served the Union in the three Indian Home Guard Regiments and 15,000 plus served the Confederacy. Indian Territory supplied a larger percentage of her population to the cause, second only to Virginia, than any other Confederate state.

    Given the task of keeping invading Federal armies out of Texas, Indian Territory suffered more destruction and loss of civilian life than any state in the Confederacy. But the Indians held the line; the Federals were never able to reach the Red River.

Unlike the rest of the Confederacy, the Indian troops became more successful after July 1863. The majority of the Indian Division of the Army of the Trans-Mississippi was still in the field and undefeated in June, 1865.

Oklahoma has recovered from the Civil War era into a modern 21st century state now. The scars from the War are lost in the passage of time. Many of the battle sites are also lost. Although a list exists (see back of book), many of them are only a memory in a book. Some have a small historical marker to designate what happened, but beyond the sign are green pastures, livestock, homes or towns. Some are covered by lakes and vacation spots. Most of the smaller sites are on private lands with no designations visible. Any remnants of the Civil War in the territory are long gone, save the forts that are designated historical sites.

The soldiers that fought and died are also a faded memory. Many of their descendents do not know they served in the Union or Confederacy, or of their sacrifices, deaths, victories or defeat. These soldiers that fought, died and survived have faded into obscurity over the 150 years since Brigadier General Stand Watie rode into Doaksville, Choctaw Nation that hot 23rd day of June, 1865 and signed the Treaty of Cease Fire with the United States of America. These are the "Forgotten Heroes, 1861-1865".

Some of the major sites, such as prominent forts, are now historical sites maintained by the federal or state governments. These host many visitors a year, with tours or re-enactments, as the public's knowledge and curiosity grows. The public is beginning to be aware that the Civil War did not just happen east of the Mississippi, it happened in Indian Territory also. The soldiers were not only white with ancestral lines stretching back to Europe, but were Native Americans, who's ancestral lines stretched back further into the mists of time than when the first white man sat foot on North American soil.

Oklahoma has a rich history that is only enhanced by the Nations that were put there against their will, but adapted, made it their home and fought for the principles they believed in. As more people research their family, they become aware they have an Indian ancestor. Now, this is a measure of pride and not hidden as so many of the great grandparents, great, great grandparents did, in order to survive in a white society.

Chapter One

1861

As the secessions started in 1861, the Cherokee Nations, both in the east and the west found themselves caught in the middle.

The Cherokee were generally Southerners by heritage, having grown up under the system of Negro slavery on plantations and small farms. Before being forced from their ancestral homes in Alabama, Georgia, North Carolina, Kentucky, and Tennessee, the Cherokee lived in villages as bands of hunters and farmers, united for mutual protection. They had developed laws, courts systems, schools and their language had become written. Among their neighbors were Creek, Choctaw and Chickasaw.

With the formation of the Confederate States of America, and the firing on Fort Sumter in Charleston Harbor, in early 1861, the Civilized Nations were caught between the two warring sides. The internal conflicts that festered just below the surface could easily erupt into a civil war.

Although politically divided because of the Removal some thirty years before, the Cherokee Nation seemed to be calm on the surface; however the old hatreds still lived down deep. The two prominent figures of the Cherokee Nation West were John Ross, the elected Principal Chief, who was 1/8 Cherokee, and Stand Watie, a 3/4 Cherokee. Watie was a member of the Ridge family who signed the Treaty of New Echota, which gave away the Cherokee lands in the east. Ross was pro-Union, even though he owned 100 slaves to work his large plantation, and Watie had strong Southern sympathies.

Watie could see the sinister shadows creeping out of the East and North toward Indian Territory. Men had fought in the Territory before, in the feuds between Watie's group and the Ross clan. However, there was something much more ominous to these shadows, as if the rising sun filled with blood, spilling out over the Indian lands. Coming on the red rays of sunrise, the dogs of war were howling, and they were growing nearer.

Stand Watie was not the only Cherokee leader worried by these developments. Old Chief John Ross worried about the effect the conflicting political philosophies of the North and the South would have on the Indian Territory. Fortune had been good to the old chief, who, though he headed the full bloods, had a Scots father and a quarter blood mother. John Ross had been born in 1790 near Lookout Mountain in Tennessee and had far less Indian blood in him than Watie. Because of these political differences, the full bloods believed that no bullet ever fired by them could kill Stand Watie! As far as Watie was concerned, the Yankees could think the same thing!

Governor Rector of Arkansas wrote Chief Ross on January 29, 1861 requesting the cooperation of the Cherokees with the Confederacy:

OFFICE SUPERINTENDENT INDIAN AFFAIRS,
Fort Smith, February 14, 1861.
Hon. JOHN ROSS,
Chief of Cherokee Nation, Tahlequah, C. N.:

SIR:
Colonel Gaines, aide-de-camp to his Excellency Governor Rector will hand you this letter. The object of Colonel Gaines' visit to you is fully explained in the letter he bears to you from the governor. I fully approve of the object the governor has in view, and would ask that you give the matter your favorable consideration.

Very respectfully, your obedient servant,
ELIAS RECTOR.
Superintendent Indian Affairs.
[Enclosure.]

THE STATE OF ARKANSAS,
EXECUTIVE DEPARTMENT,
Little Rock, January 29, 1861.

To His Excellency JOHN ROSS, Principal Chief Cherokee Nation:

SIR:
It may now be regarded as almost certain that the States having slave property within their borders will, in consequence of repeated northern aggressions, separate themselves and withdraw from the Federal Government. South Carolina, Alabama, Florida, Mississippi, Georgia, and Louisiana have already, by action of the people, assumed this attitude. Arkansas, Missouri, Tennessee, Kentucky, Virginia, North Carolina, and Maryland will probably pursue the same course by the 4th of March next. Your people, in their institutions, productions, latitude, and natural sympathies, are allied to the common brotherhood of the slaveholding States. Our people and yours are natural allies in war and friends in peace. Your country is salubrious and fertile, and possesses the highest capacity for future progress and development by the application of slave labor. Besides this, the contiguity of our territory with yours induces relations of so intimate a character as to preclude the idea of discordant or separate action.

It is well established that the Indian country west of Arkansas is looked to by the incoming administration of Mr. Lincoln as fruitful fields, ripe for the harvest of abolitionism, free soilers, and Northern mountebanks. We hope to find in your people friends willing to co-operate with the South in defense of her institutions, her honor, and her firesides, and with whom the slaveholding States are willing to share a common future, and to afford protection commensurate with your exposed condition and your subsisting monetary interests with the General Government.

As a direct means of expressing to you these sentiments, I have dispatched my aide-de-camp, Lieut. Col. J. J. Gaines, to confer with you confidentially upon these subjects, and to report to me any expressions of kindness and confidence that you may see proper to communicate to the governor of Arkansas, who is your friend and the friend of your people.

Respectfully, your obedient servant,
HENRY M. RECTOR,
Governor of Arkansas.

The Chief answered, stating the Cherokee would remain neutral. He stated that the quarrel between the states did not concern the Indians. He followed this up by letters of May 17, June 12 and 17 and in a proclamation on May 17 that repeated his stand for this principle.

On January 5, 1861, the Chickasaw Legislature discussed setting up an intertribal conference so the Civilized Nations could discuss and arrive at some mutual action regarding the coming split between the North and South. Chickasaw Governor sent out a plan to the other tribes and the Creek chiefs named a conference for February 17.

On February 7, the Choctaw Nation came out for the slave states. They stated, "Their natural affection, education, institutions, and interests bound them in every way to the destiny of their neighbors and brothers of the Southern states. The Choctaw Nation had 5,000 Negro slaves.

On February 9, Jefferson Davis became President of the Confederacy and 8 days later, the leaders in the Territory met at their conference as the Creeks had proposed. They decided to follow John Ross's course and remain neutral, at least for the time being. The Congress of the Confederate States began at once to establish procedures to build an agency system among the Five Civilized Tribes. On February 20, section two of a bill that created the Confederate War Department placed the care of the Indians under the Secretary of War. Here they remained until the Bureau of Indian Affairs was created March 14, 1861, when. David Hubbard of Alabama became the first appointed Confederate Commissioner of Indian Affairs.

As early as February, the Southern States began seizing United States arsenals within their borders, securing weapons, powder, and supplies for the military. Since many of the cabinet members in the Buchanan Administration were Southern men, they did little or nothing to stop the states from seizing the arsenals, forts, and military posts. The ordinance, quartermaster and commissary supplies would be valuable, and they were resigning their positions when the new administration of Lincoln came into power. Both the Union and Confederate authorities felt the difficulty of securing arms and equipment in this early period of the war for the new troops called up.

The plains Indians and the Five Nations sent delegates to Antelope Hills in western Indian Territory, to meet and discuss the growing unrest. Antelope Hills lies in a bend of the Canadian River in present day Roger Mills County near the Oklahoma - Texas State line. Chief Ross's delegates encouraged neutrality and wanted to develop plans for all Indians to take advantage of the white man's problems to strengthen

Indian Sovereignty. They were hoping to build a strong Indian Confederacy. However, there was division among the delegates gathered the same that had divided the States.

The Creek Chief, O-Pothle-yohola, rode into the western country with some of his men to attend the meeting. With him were other leaders, White King and Sands, and headmen from the Cherokee and Chickasaw Nations. As he rode, O-Pothle-yohola spoke to many nations, urging them to stand with him in the coming war. It was not their fight; it was the white man's. Let the white men kill each other until the grounds ran red with their blood. Let the tribes unite as one, stand together, as brothers of the same fire, and shun the white man's war. Wherever they went it was the same, some listened, others walked away.

The western land of Antelope Hills was wild and windswept, antelope replaced the deer, dry gullies and ravines replaced streams. It was a dry, drought-stricken country, this "Far West lands," where grass and insects struggled to live. However, this was home for the most fearsome of the plains Nations, the "Komantsi" (Comanche). Entire countries trembled at their name; savages like the Texans feared them instinctively, and even those in a far-away place called Mexico lived in terror of their raids. If O-pothle-yahola could persuade the Komantsi to join the Muskogee, no amount of evil could destroy them. A few of the Comanche listened and believed, but the rest were unmoved. The Comanche feared no one and saw no reason to join others for protection. Then they rode away, disappearing into the distant haze of the plains.

Slowly, spring came that year, sliding its silken glove over the hills and valleys of Indian Territory. Rains had brought the flowers in the meadows, leaves burst forth, and the country came alive. Perhaps the drought that had gripped the region in 1860 would end.

The dark cloak of impending war still hovered among the people. Already states in the east were withdrawing from the Union and forming a new Republic, the Confederate States of America. It would not be long now.

Military conflict between the Northern and Southern States erupted at Fort Sumter, South Carolina, April 12, 1861. Before that date, however, agents from Arkansas and Texas had converged on Indian Territory to persuade the Tribes to join with the Confederate States of America. The Federal Army moved out of the forts in Indian Territory. Federal posts at Fort Smith and Little Rock, Arkansas, and Texas became the possessions of the Confederates without a fight. The Confederates moved swiftly to consolidate their hold on Indian Territory. Texas troops rode into the area in April to occupy Forts Washita, Arbuckle, and Cobb, without firing a shot. The small Federal garrison forces had been recalled for service in the East. However, the Indian Nations are not important enough to leave a Federal representation there; after all, they were not really "people." Besides, the troops were needed for the bigger war in the east.

Pro Northern and Pro-Union Indians felt betrayed by the withdrawal of the Regular Army from the forts in Indian Territory. The Nations had been promised protection from the 'wild Plains Indians" when they had been forced to agree to move west of the Mississippi. Suddenly, their defenders were gone and there was fear and resentment among the Nations.

Accompanying the withdrawal of the United States troops were other disturbing events. Several of the most trusted and known Federal Indian Agents, for instance, Douglas H. Cooper, left to serve the Confederacy. In addition, of course, money owed the tribes by the Federal government for sale of their old lands was suspended. The U.S. was afraid that the shipments would be seized by Arkansas or Texas, just another item that added to the Indians growing sense of betrayal.

The strip of land extending from the Missouri-Kansas border, westward along the southern Kansas border, known as the Neutral Lands. It was wedge shaped, 50 miles wide at the eastern end, and connecting at a zero point at the west, covering several counties. This land belonged to the Cherokee under a treaty but very few Indians and some white settlers (squatters) lived there in 1860. It made an effective barrier that kept Union agents from going into the Nations to work for the Union cause. The flames of secession spread and southern agents had already been sent into the Territory.

The Confederacy had a different view of the Nations. The Southern Superintendency took in South Kansas and the whole of Indian Territory (now Oklahoma). In the Nations were the five great slave holding tribes that had come from south of the Mason-Dixon line; the Cherokee, Choctaw, Chickasaw, Creek and Seminole, some New York Indian families, Quapaws, Caddos, Shawnees, and Senecas, as well as some exiled Texas Indians. In the same geographic group were the Black Dog Tribe of the Osage of Southern Kansas, which supported secession along with some of the wild Plains Tribes and the half-wild Wichitas.

The Central Agency north of the 37th parallel was loyal. They included the Sac and Fox, Munsee, Delaware, Shawnee, Weas, Peories, Kaskaskia, Piankeshaw, Potawatomie, Ottawa, Miami, Chippawa and Kaw of North central Kansas. This Agency's tribes were from Free states and they stood by the Union. More than half of the adult males of the Delaware enlisted as volunteers and some would die under Stand Watie's guns.

Confederate Indian Commissioner, Albert Pike, became the key player in the political chaos of Indian Territory in 1861. Pike was born in Massachusetts, an attorney and a poet. He was one of the few whites that knew some Southern Indian languages. He impressed the Nations with his dignity, eloquence, and proven interest in their culture and well-being and he had recently won a major financial settlement for the Creek Nation.

Pike left Arkansas in May 1861, with a wagon train loaded with potted food, wine, provisions for comfort, and various trade goods, on his mission to secure Indian Territory for the Confederacy. He had been authorized by the Confederate Government to spend $100,000.00 for treaties of alliance with the tribes there.

Before he left, on May 11, Pike had written a letter stating:

"I foresaw some time ago that the regular troops would be withdrawn, as too much needed elsewhere to be left inactive, and that they would be replaced by volunteers, under men actuated by personal hatred of the South. I do not think that more than five or six thousand men will be sent there (Indian Territory) for a time, but those, I am satisfied, will be there soon. To occupy the country with safety, we ought to have at least an equal force, if we first occupy it, and shall need a much larger one if they establish themselves during an inaction. It will hardly be safe to count upon putting in the field more than 3,500 Indians; maybe we may get 5,000. To procure any, or at least any respectable number, we must guarantee them their lands, annuities and other rights under treaties, furnish them arms (rifles and revolvers, if the latter can be had), advance them some $25.00 a head in cash, and send them a respectable force there, as evidence that they will be efficiently seconded by us."

While visiting the Indian Nations, word came from the east of the Confederate's first major battle win at Manassas on July 21, 1861.

When O-pothle-yohola returned from the plains, there was more bad news. As in the past, the McIntosh had betrayed the People and joined the Confederate States and half the Creek towns had followed. At a quickly called meeting, at the Council Grounds, the McIntosh and the rest who had signed a Confederate treaty declared they spoke for no one but themselves.

Since the Removal, years earlier, a functional balance of power in the Creek Nation had been developed between supporters of O-pothle-yohola, and those of Daniel N. McIntosh, the son of William McIntosh, of the Lower Towns. William McIntosh had fought with the U. S. in the Creek War, 1813-1814, and had signed the treaty removing the Creeks to Indian Territory in 1825. The McIntosh faction, more like the Southern white society, had Southern sympathies, while O-pothle-yohola, a traditionalist of the Creek culture and religion, had never forgiven the Southern States for their part in the Indian Removal.

The Creek delegates strongly favored the United States. John Ross had urged O-pothle-yohola to remain neutral. After the meeting, plans were made to head north into Cherokee Country across the Arkansas, where they would join up with the Cherokee and the Union forces. Then came more news! While they were getting ready to move to the Arkansas, a rider came in with the news that John Ross and the Cherokees had allied with the Confederates. It did not matter the reason, all that mattered was the Muskogee were betrayed by John Ross's Cherokee! The only option was to ally with the Federal Government and somehow reach Northern troops coming from Kansas before the McIntosh and the Confederates overtook them.

Chief Moty Kinnard and the McIntosh created a Creek Confederate Military Unit, the First Creek Regiment, organized by McIntosh, August 19, 1861. Many of the officers and men were relatives of the McIntosh family, and many were descendents of Lower vs. Upper Creeks. The unit also contained some Seminole. Daniel's brother, Chilly, left the unit and organized a new one, the Creek Battalion, in fall 1861, which became the Second Creek Regiment in 1862.

As neighboring tribes came under the Confederate Flag, the pressure grew on the Cherokee to declare for the South. Representatives of the Tribes met at North Fork Town on July 1, 1861, and organized the United Nations of the Indian Territory, and shortly thereafter, they signed treaties with the Confederate commissioner, Albert Pike.

In July, Stand Watie, the political opponent of Chief Ross, organized his regiment of mixed bloods to cooperate with the Confederacy. General Ben McCulloch, Confederate Commander in Arkansas commissioned Watie a Colonel in the Confederate Provisional Army. Short and stocky, legs bowed by many years riding horses, Watie was 3/4 Cherokee, but looked full blood. At 55 years, he was a born leader. He was a quiet man, who seldom spoke, but, when he did, people listened. He had the qualities of leadership, and such respect from his troops that they followed where he led.

Officers of Watie's Regiment was Captain: Stand Watie; First Lt.: Buzzard; Second Lt. Wilson Saugee; Third Lt. Charles Edwin Watie; Orderly Sergeant Henry Forrester. Most of the officers and a number of the enlisted men were not full Cherokee by birth. In addition, because of many social and economic connections between the regiments officers and citizens of neighboring states, the organization contained white recruits from northwestern Arkansas and southwestern Missouri. Watie's regiment would remain completely faithful to him and the Confederacy, serving the duration of the war. The regiment would be with him in Doaksville, June 23, 1865, when he signed the cease-fire

They served in the Delaware District and Neutral Land, which was a legal part of that district. Other companies were formed, and met near Fort Wayne on July 12, 1861, to form the Cherokee Mounted Rifle Regiment. Joel Mayes Bryan organized and became Major of Bryan's Battalion. The Second Mounted Volunteers was formed. Moses Frye organized and became Major of Frye's Battalion. Joseph Absalom Scales later succeeded him. The officers elected were Colonel: Stand Watie; Lt. Colonel: Thomas Fox Taylor; Major: Elias Cornelius Boudinot; Adjutant: Charles E. Watie; Quarter Master: George Washington Adair; Commissary: Joseph McMinn Starr, Sr.; Surgeons: Drs. Walter Thompson Adair and William Davis Polson; Chaplain: C. M. Slover; Sergeant Majors: George West and Joseph Franklin Thompson

Ratified on July 20 by council, the treaty with the Creek divided the people into "Southern" and "Northern" factions of almost equal numbers. Chiefs Moty Kennard, Echo Harjo, Chilly, and D. N. McIntosh led the Southern Creek. The Loyals who where largely full bloods, were led by O-pothle-yoholo and Sands. The Southern Creeks organized a Confederate Regiment. It included the First Creek Cavalry, under Col. Daniel N. McIntosh, their War Chief, a mixed unit of Creek and Seminole, the First Seminole Cavalry Battalion with Major John Jumper, a Seminole, as second in Command, under Lt. Col. Chilly McIntosh, and an independent company under Captain James M. C. Smith. The Choctaw and Chickasaw Warriors organized into the First Regiment Choctaw and Chickasaw Mounted Rifles under Colonel Douglas Cooper, a former U.S. Indian agent, veteran of the Mexican War, and Second in Command under Brigadier General Albert Pike. Of the almost 18,000 Choctaw, all but about 300 had gone with the Secessionist South.

On May 25, the Chickasaw Legislature announced its support of the Confederacy, and urged the neighboring Tribes to "form an alliance against the Lincoln hordes and Kansas robbers against who will wage a war against their Southern friends, which would surpass the French Revolution in scenes of blood and horror."

With the division in the Cherokee, many wanted to follow friends and remain pro-Union, or at least, neutral. Chief Ross's second wife, Mary B. Stapler, was a Quaker from Delaware. Her family was in the North and he did not want to alienate them. Some Cherokee disliked Southerners because they took their lands when they were forced to move to Indian Territory. Other Cherokee disliked Texans because some had attacked several Cherokee settlements in Texas. Moreover, civil war was about to erupt between the Ross and Ridge parties as old hatreds flared again. Even Northern politicians made the Cherokee uneasy. William Seward, in a speech during the 1860 election stated; "All Indian Territory south of Kansas must be vacated by the Indians." Southern secessionists claimed the abolitionists of the North wanted the Indians' land for greedy white farmers. When Seward became Secretary of State, some Indians feared another Trail of Tears.

The summer grew hot, the drought still in the country. As the controversy raged in the Five Tribes as to which side to ally with, Pike made sure he covered everything. He journeyed on west, and August 12, 1861, completed treaties with the Kiowa, Comanche, Wichita, Arapaho, Caddo, and Tonkawa at Fort Arbuckle. Unlike the treaties with the Five Tribes, the Treaties with the plains tribes did not involve military service. He promised the Confederacy would provided an annual ration of food, livestock, tools and other goods, so the chiefs put their mark on the treaties. As long as they left the Confederates alone, and did not raid into the Confederate ally, Texas, their lives would not change. With these preliminary arrangements made, Pike promised to return in 1862, after the Confederacy approved the terms of the treaty. He wrote enthusiastic letters to his superiors concerning his work, even sending letters to Jefferson Davis himself.

In spite of General Pike's efforts, things did not go well at Fort Cobb. Towasi (Silver Broach) and Esa-Havey were first and second chiefs of the Penateka Comanche. They were friendly to the whites and gave no trouble. The third chief, however, was Buffalo Hump. His disposition had not improved since the troublesome times in Texas. He told Matthew Leeper that he wanted a house because he intended to settle down. Leeper did not intend to build a house for any Indian, and told Buffalo Hump so in undiplomatic terms. Buffalo Hump let his young men create mischief around the agency and he quarreled with Horace Jones. Leeper was a contrary person and had differences with his subordinate Sturm and with his superior, Elis Rector. Mr. Rector rebuked him, as did Pike. They even placed him under arrest, but later released him. Then Rector and Pike quarreled, and Pike quarreled with the department head, General Hindman.

All this had a bad effect on the Indians. The Caddos and Tonkawas showed signs of shifting their allegiance to the Federals. The Delaware already sympathized with the Union. The Penatekas did not care who won the war, as long as they were fed!

Under the treaties, the Confederacy provided for a courts system for the Indians in which they had the same rights and privileges as the white citizens of the Confederacy, on equal terms with the other Southern states' systems. Until these court systems were in place, the Indians would be under the jurisdiction of the District Court of Western Arkansas. The Indians would have control over their courts, as the treaties greatly increased the legal rights of the Indians. The actions by the South virtually ended all discrimination based on Indian blood within the Confederate Court system.

The Tribes did not have to pay taxes in their association with the Confederacy, and were guaranteed they would not have to pay any of the war debts incurred by the South. Since the Indians did not tax themselves, they relied on the revenue raising measures allowed in the treaties.

They were allowed to tax all licensed white traders bringing goods into the Territory. This import tax, based on the initial cost of the goods, was not to exceed 1- 1/4 per cent. Citizens of the Territory did not need a license. In addition, they could charge $1.00 per head for cattle grazed on their land.

The main income for the Nations was the annuities paid by the Confederate government. Yearly annuities for the Creeks were $24,500.00; Choctaws, $9,000.00; Chickasaws, $3,000.00; Seminoles, $25,000.00 and the Cherokee $10,000.00. The Nations also received money for schools, blacksmith facilities, and to help increase agricultural production. The Creeks received $7,000 for Education, $7,640 for agriculture and blacksmith shops, and $38,820.00 for interest on their bonds, making the total paid to the Creeks by the South, $71,960.00. The other Nations received the same special allotments.

The Choctaws received $600.00 for the support of their Light Horseman, $600.00 for blacksmiths, $320.00 instead of the permanent provision for iron and steel development, and $25,000.00 in interest, making their total $35,520.00. The Chickasaws were entitled to $2,616.89 in various allotments, in addition to sharing in the special allotments of the Choctaw. The Seminole were paid $3,000.00 for their schools, $2,200 for agriculture, $2,200 for blacksmiths, plus an additional $1,000 to build two schoolhouses. The Cherokee received $4,500.00 for a permanent orphan fund, $17,772 for education, and $43,372.36 interest on state bonds, plus $5,000.00 a year interest on their orphan fund.

The aid the Confederacy promised the Indians would have been very beneficial, if they had been able to live up to their commitments. As the war progressed, the South began to default on the annuity payments. This caused much dissatisfaction among the Indians.

The treaties allowed the Nations to be represented in the Confederate Congress. The Creek and Seminole had one joint representative, Choctaw and Chickasaw had one, elected alternately between the two Nations and the Cherokee one representative. They would serve two-year terms, had to be 21 years old and under no legal disability. The Creek and Seminole delegate had to be a member of one of those Nations. The Cherokee delegate had to be a native born citizen, and the Choctaw and Chickasaw delegate had to be a tribal member either on father's or mother's side. The delegates elected to the Confederate House of Representatives were Robert M. Jones, Choctaw, representing the Choctaw and Chickasaw Nations, Elias Cornelius Boudinot, Cherokee and S. B. Callahan, Creek and Seminole.

Wilson's Creek, Missouri

General Nathaniel Lyons, an abolitionist, had advanced the Union banner during the summer in Missouri. He had walked over all his opposition from St. Louis to Jefferson City, Boonville, and Springfield in a contest for Missouri. The capitol, Jefferson City, fell without a fight and Governor Jackson and the pro-Confederate government had fled with the state archives. Lyon soon learned the Missourians had rallied at Boonville, but the untrained soldiers, under young Colonel John S. Marmaduke were no match for the regulars.

Governor Jackson and his government, some 4,000 state officials and Southerners, retreated south, gathering allies along the way. Wealthy Jo Shelby and Senator James Rains joined Jackson's "Army" without uniforms, flying the Confederate flag on the flanks and the Missouri flag at the center, with 3,000 volunteers and 3 guns manned by Hiram Bledsoe, sporting his sweeping mustache and goatee. The army stopped its march at Carthage to engage General Franz Sigel. Lyon was defeated and pulled back to Springfield. He had hoped to overcome Jackson before he joined forces with Sterling Price and Benjamin McCulloch.

Stand Watie's battalion of 300 Confederate Cherokee, stationed near the Arkansas-Cherokee Nation border, scouted into Missouri and Kansas to keep Jayhawkers and Kansas abolitionists out of the Cherokee Nation. A contingent of Cherokee participated in the important Confederate victory, August 10, 1861 at the Battle of Wilson's Creek, or Oak Hills, just southwest of Springfield. Joel Mayes, a well-known Cherokee cattleman, was Captain of a Cherokee company scouting for Brig. General Ben McCulloch's Confederate Army of Arkansas, Louisiana, Missouri, and Texas. Mayes and his men were a part of Watie's battalion. There were an estimated almost 1,000 Cherokee and Choctaw in the battle.

On the Southern side, besides Generals McCulloch and Price, were Jo Shelby and his cavalry, Charles Quantrill, who commanded a group of mixed bloods from the Territory, and Coleman and James Younger, who later gained a name fighting under Quantrill's guerilla banner. On the Northern side, was a fellow named "Wild" Bill Hickock, in his high-heeled boots and fresh from the Kansas cattle wars.

These Confederate Warriors were with the third Louisiana Infantry as they charged the German-American troops under Colonel Franz Siegal, who had attacked McCulloch's camp. They over ran Siegel's artillery, capturing several pieces of artillery, then moved through the clouds of gun smoke toward the north end of the camp, where the Union's main force, under Brigadier General Nathaniel Lyon was desperately holding a small ridge. His hard-fisted surprise attack stalled before a murderous Rebel artillery barrage.

Although General Lyon held the high ground, he was outnumbered. Frantically, he rallied his second Kansas Volunteer Infantry for a counter attack. As they marched across a stretch of open ground toward the Rebels, sudden gunfire erupted at close range in front of the column. Mayes' Cherokee company had moved unseen into the bushes close to the Union line. The shocking hail of deadly lead took its toll, knocking Lyon from his horse, to become the first Union General killed in action in the Civil War. The report after the battle of Wilson's Creek stated some of the Union troops were found scalped and Captain Mayes' Cherokees were the prime suspects.

Casualties at Wilson's Creek were about 23 percent of all engaged. The Federals fell back to Springfield, and that evening, General McCulloch sent the body of General Lyon, forgotten in the retreat, to the Federal lines. Fearing another attack the Federals pulled back to Rolla, 175 miles away. Leaving Lyon behind, the doctors failed to inject the body with arsenic against decomposition. Mrs. John Phelps, a Union woman and senator's wife, learned of this and had his body placed in a coffin, then stored it in her outdoor cellar covered with straw. Later, fearing the Confederates would steal the body, she had it buried. Several weeks later, relatives came and were allowed through Confederate lines, to take the body back to Connecticut for burial.

Daniel O'Flaherty wrote about Wilson's Creek in his book, "General Jo Shelby - Undefeated Rebel":

"Wilson's Creek was the Bull Run of the West and its analogy to the first great battle in Virginia is remarkable.

In both cases, the battle was the first conflict on a vast scale in its particular theater of the war. In both cases the Southern troops were panicked into flight in the opening phases of the battle; in both cases they rallied to smash the enemy, hurl him back into the tight ring of defenses of his capitol; and in both cases they were so exhausted by the victory they could not follow it up. In Virginia, the Confederates lost the opportunity to march on Washington after Bull Run and perhaps end the war by dictating peace terms from the capitol. In Missouri they failed to pursue the defeated enemy after Wilson's Creek and retake the Missouri River valley, which would have brought Missouri into the orbit of the Confederacy, gained control of the vital upper Mississippi, and perhaps saved the heartland of the South from invasion.

Both Bull Run and Wilson's Creek demonstrated the fatal military weakness of the new Southern nation, its inability to make its victories count."

Chapter Two

Confederate victories at Bull Run, Virginia July 22 and Wilson's Creek, Missouri, August 10, near the Cherokee Nation, forced the Cherokee Nation to take a hard look at their neutrality. The Union forces had been defeated with thousands killed or wounded and had to pull back to their base of operation. This gave the Confederacy prestige. Nearly all doubters believed the South would be victorious in winning her independence. The Federal Government abandoned the Nations. They had more things to worry about than a bunch of Indians west of the Mississippi. All other Indian Nations on the Cherokee borders were Confederate, Arkansas, southern Missouri, Texas was pro-Confederate, and Stand Watie was leading a battalion of Confederate Cherokee. Ross found it increasingly difficult to maintain neutrality.

Friends of the South were elated by the victories by the Confederacy. They urged the ones who were hesitating as to which side to support, to cast their lot with the Southern cause.

When the Cherokee learned of these defeats of the Union Army, Chief Ross, still at odds with his old political rival, gave in to those that urged him to sign Pike's treaty. The cunning, 72 year old politician realized that a separate treaty signed between Watie and the Confederacy would strip him of any powers as Principle chief. He also knew that the millions of dollars owed the Cherokee by the U.S. government for the "sale" of their lands in North Carolina, Georgia, Alabama and Tennessee was tied up in bonds issued in the Southern States and very likely would be canceled by the Federal government.

However, with Pike's treaty, the Confederacy would assume the Federal government's financial obligations to the tribe and even seat a Cherokee

Delegate in the Confederate Congress. The early impressive Confederate victories at Bull Run (Manassas) Virginia, and Wilson's Creek, Missouri, had convinced many in the Territory that the Confederacy would win this war, and it would be in the best interest of the tribes to be on the winning side.

The Confederate troops were active, and the Cherokee Nation was feeling more pressure, making it more and more difficult to maintain neutrality. Finally, Chief Ross relented.

On August 5, the Creek Nation held a meeting attended mostly by non-treaty people, to send delegates to Washington through the abolitionist Kansas leaders. O-pothle-yoholo writes to President Lincoln on August 15,

"Now I write the President, Our Great Father who removed us to our present home and made a treaty, and you said that in our new homes we should be defended from all interference from any person and that no white people in the whole world would ever molest us, but that the land would be ours as long as the grass grows and the waters run.....But now the wolf has come. Men who are strangers tread our soil. Our children are frightened and the mothers can not sleep for fear. This is our situation now. When we made our treaty at Washington... we believed you. Then our Great Father was strong. Now White people are trying to take our people away to fight against us and you. I am alive. I well remember the treaty. My ears are open and my memory is good."

Chief Ross called a general convention of the Cherokees to meet at Tahlequah on August 21, 1861. Four thousand Cherokees gathered at Tahlequah, filed up to the Council house and pitched their tents in wind-sheltered valleys. John Ross and his brother,

Lewis, the Cherokee treasurer, spoke to the crowd, asking for a Confederate alliance. The frock coated "white" mixed bloods did not oppose the chief, since this time, he had switched to Watie's position. However, what of the full bloods in turbans and calico shirts, men who looked no part of the Southern civilization, as did their half blood brothers with their fair Anglo wives.

The assembled Cherokees gave the answer, union with the Confederacy and the raising of a regiment by the Cherokee Executive Committee, for "national defense" that would be designated the First Cherokee Mounted Rifles, even though, Watie had formed the first Cherokee regiment. Stand Watie's independent command was already in high standing in Confederate circles.

With John Drew, a wealthy salt works owner as Colonel enrolled the Regiment on October 4 1861. Though related to Ross by marriage, he was respected by the Ridge-Watie faction, and like Watie, was pro-Confederate and mixed blood. Many of Drew's troops were of full blood Cherokee; many were members of the Keetoowah Society and/or the Loyal League, a group that considered anyone who signed the removal treaty a traitor.

The Chief wrote General McCulloch that:

"We are authorized to form an alliance with the Confederate States, which we are determined to do as early as practicable. This determination may give rise to movements against the Cherokee people upon their northern border. To be prepared for any such emergency, we have deemed it prudent to proceed to organize a regiment of mounted men and tender them for service. They will be raised forthwith, by Colonel John Drew, and if received by you, will require to be armed."

McCulloch, replying to John Ross' letter of alliance said:

"Permit me to congratulate you upon the course you have thought proper to pursue. The people of the Confederate States and those of the Cherokee Nation must share a common destiny. Their interests and institutions are the same. Then, let us as brothers cooperate against a common enemy to us and those institutions, and drive them form our borders whenever they dare approach them."

On the surface, the warring factions of the Cherokee Nation appeared united. However, McCulloch, in late September, warned Pike to separate the Indian commands under Watie and Drew because of the inevitable clash if they encountered each other. General McCulloch had reported to the Confederate Government, that nearly all the full bloods and many of the half blood Cherokee under Chief Ross were against slavery and it would be a safe bet they would show their true colors when they could do so with reasonable safety.

Time moved into fall, and the weather cooled, as the war heated up. On October 7, Pike had arrived to sign the treaties. He presented Colonel Drew with a flag and helped Chief Ross write the Cherokee Declaration of Independence. The treaty said in part; "The Confederate States of America having accepted the said protectorate, hereby solemnly promises the said Cherokee Nation never to desert or abandon it, and that under no circumstances will they permit the Northern States, or any other enemy to overcome them and sever the Cherokees from the Confederacy; but that they will, at any cost and all hazards, protect and defend them, and maintain unbroken ties created by identity of interests and institutions, and strengthened and made perpetual by this treaty."

Ross delivered this message to the National Council to his people on October 9, 1861

MESSAGE OF THE PRINCIPAL CHIEF TO THE CHEROKEE NATION

To the National Committee and Council:
"Friends and Fellow Council:"

"Since the last meeting of the National Council, events have occurred that will occupy prominent place in the history of the world. The United States have been dissolved and two governments now exist. Twelve of the states composing the late Union, have erected themselves into a government, under the style of the Confederate States of America, and, as you know, are now engaged in a war for their independence.

The contest, thus far, has been attended with success almost uninterrupted on their side and marked by brilliant victories. Of its final result, there seems to be no grounds for a reasonable doubt. The unanimity and devotion of the people of the Confederate States must sooner or later secure their success over all opposition and result in the establishment of their independence and a recognition of it by the other nations of the earth.

At the beginning of the conflict, I felt that the Interest of the Cherokee people would be best maintained by remaining quiet and not involving themselves in it prematurely. Our relations had long existed with the United States Government and bound us to amity and peace alike with all the States. Neutrality was proper and wise so long as there remained a reasonable probability that the difficulty between the two sections of the Union would be settled, as a different course would have

But, when there was no longer any reason to believe that the Union of the States would be continued, there was no cause to hesitate as to the course the Cherokee Nation should pursue. Our geographical position and domestic institutions allied us to the South. While the developments daily made in our vicinity, and as to the purposes of the war waged against the Confederate States, clearly pointed out the path of our interest.

These considerations produced a unanimity of sentiment among the people as to the policy adopted by the Cherokee Nation, which was clearly expressed in their general meeting held at Tahlequah on the 21st of August last. A copy of the proceedings of that meeting is submitted for your information.

In accordance with the declarations embodied in the resolutions then adopted, the Executive Council deemed it proper to exercise the authority conferred upon them by the people there assembled. Messengers dispatched to General Albert Pike, the distinguished Indian Commissioner of the Confederate States, who having negotiated treaties with the neighboring Indian nations, was then establishing relations between his government and the Comanches and other Indians in the Southwest, who bore a copy of the proceedings of the meeting referred to, and a letter from the executive authorities, proposing on behalf of the nation to enter into a treaty of alliance, defensive and offensive, with the Confederate States.

In the exercise of the same general authority, and to be ready as far as practicable to meet any emergency that might spring up on our northern border, it was thought proper to raise a regiment of mounted men and tender its services to General McCullough. The people responded with alacrity to the call, and it is believed the regiment will be found as efficient as any other like number of men. It is now in the service of the Confederate States for the purpose of aiding in defending their homes and the common rights of the Indian Nations about us.

This regiment is composed of ten full companies, with two reserve companies, and, in addition to the force previously authorized to be raised, to operate outside of the Nation by General McCullough, will show that the Cherokee people are ready to do all in their power in defense of the Confederate cause, which has now become our own. And, it is to be hoped that our people will spare no means to sustain them, but contribute liberally to supply any want of comfortable clothing for the approaching season.

In years long since past, our ancestors undaunted those who would invade their mountain homes beyond the Mississippi. Let not their descendants of the present day be found unworthy of them, or unable to stand by the chivalrous men of the South, by whose side they may be called to fight in self-defense. The Cherokee people do not desire to be involved in war, but, self-preservation fully justifies them in the course they have adopted, and they will be recreant to themselves if they should not sustain it to the utmost of their humble abilities.

A treaty with the Confederate States has been entered into and is now submitted for your ratification. In view of the circumstances by which we are surrounded, and the provisions of the treaty, it will be found to be the most important ever negotiated on behalf of the Cherokee Nation, and will mark a new era in its history. Without attempting a recapitulation of all its provisions, some of its distinguishing features may be briefly enumerated.

The relations of the Cherokee Nation are changed from the United, to the Confederate States, with guarantees of protection and a recognition in future negotiations only of its constitutional authorities. The metes and boundaries, as defined by patent from the United States, are continued, and a guarantee given for the Neutral Land or a fair consideration in case it should be lost by war or negotiation, and an advance thereon, to pay the national debt and to meet other contingencies. The payment of all our annuities and security of all our investments are provided for. The jurisdiction of the Cherokee courts over all members of the Nation, whether by birth, marriage, or adoption, is recognized.

Our title to our lands is placed beyond dispute. Our relations with the Confederate States is that of a ward; theirs to us that of a protectorate, with powers restricted. The district court, with a limited civil and criminal jurisdiction, is admitted into the country instead of being located at Van Buren, as was the United States court. This is perhaps one of the most important provisions of the treaty, and secures to our citizens the great constitutional right of trial by a jury of their own vicinage, and releases them from the petty abuses and vexations of the old system, before a foreign jury and in a foreign country. It gives us a delegate in congress on the same footing with delegates from the Territories, by which our interests can be represented; a right which has long been withheld from the Nation and which has imposed upon it a large expense and a great injustice. It also contains reasonable stipulation in regard to the appointing powers of the Agent and in regard to licensed traders. The Cherokee Nation may be called upon to furnish troops for the defense of the Indian country, but is never to be taxed for the support of any war in which the States may be engaged.

The Cherokee people stand upon new ground. Let us hope that the clouds which overspread the land will be dispersed and that we shall prosper as we have never before done. New avenues of usefulness and distinction will be open to the ingenious youth of the country. Our rights of self-government will be more fully recognized, and our citizens will be no longer dragged off upon flimsy pretexts, to be imprisoned and tried before distant tribunals. No just cause exists for domestic difficulties. Let them be buried with the past and only mutual friendship and harmony be cherished.

Our relations with the neighboring tribes are of the most friendly character. Let us see that the white path which leads from our country to theirs be obstructed by no act of ours, and that it be open to all those with whom we may be brought into intercourse.

Amid the excitement of the times it is to be hoped that the interests of education will not be allowed to suffer and that no interruption be brought into the usual operations of the government. Let its officers continue to discharge their appropriate duties. As the services of some of your members may be required elsewhere and all unnecessary expense should be avoided, I respectfully recommend that the business of the session be promptly discharged."

    John Ross.
    Executive Department,
    Tahlequah, C. N.,
    October 9, 1861"

On October 28th, 1861, the Cherokee National Council issued the following declaration:

"DECLARATION BY THE PEOPLE OF THE CHEROKEE NATION OF THE CAUSES WHICH HAVE IMPELLED THEM TO UNITE THEIR FORTUNES WITH THOSE OF THE CONFEDERATE STATES OF AMERICA."

"When circumstances beyond their control compel one people to sever the ties which have long existed between them and another state or confederacy, and to contract new alliances and establish new relations for the security of their rights and liberties, it is fit that they should publicly declare the reasons by which their action is justified.

The Cherokee people had its origin in the South; its institutions are similar to those of the Southern States, and their interests identical with theirs. Long since it accepted the protection of the United States of America, contracted with them treaties of alliance and friendship, and allowed themselves to be to a great extent governed by their laws.

In peace and war, they have been faithful to their engagements with the United States. With much hardship and injustice to complain of, they resorted to no other means than solicitation and argument to obtain redress. Loyal and obedient to the laws and the stipulations of the treaties, they served under the flag of the United States, shared the common dangers, and were entitled to a share in the common glory, to gain which their blood was freely shed on the battlefield.

When the dissension between the Southern and Northern States culminated in a separation of State after State from the Union, they watched the progress of events with anxiety and consternation. While their institutions and the contiguity of their territory to the states of Arkansas, Texas and Missouri made the cause of the seceding States necessarily their own cause, their treaties had been made with the United States, and they felt the utmost reluctance even in appearance to violate their engagements or set at naught the obligations of good faith.

Conscious that they were a people few in numbers compared with either of the contending parties, and that their country might with no considerable force be easily overrun and devastated and desolation and ruin be the result if they took up arms for either side, their authorities determined that no other course was consistent with the dictates of prudence or could secure the safety of their people and immunity from the horrors of a war waged by an invading enemy than a strict neutrality, and in this decision they were sustained by a majority of the Nation.

That policy was accordingly adopted and faithfully adhered to. Early in the month of June of the present year the authorities of the Nation declined to enter into negotiations for an alliance with the Confederate States, and protested against the occupation of the Cherokee country by their troops, or any other violation of their neutrality. No act was allowed that could be construed by the United States to be a violation of the faith of treaties.

But Providence rules the destinies of nations, and events, by inexorable necessity, overrule human resolutions. The number of the Confederate States increased to eleven, and their government is firmly established and consolidated. Maintaining in the field an army of two hundred thousand men, the war became for them but a succession of victories. Disclaiming any intention to invade the Northern States, they sought only to repel invaders from their own soil and to secure the right of governing themselves.

They claimed only the privilege asserted by the Declaration of American Independence, and on which the right of the Northern States themselves to self-government is formed, of altering their form of government when it became no longer tolerable and establishing new forms for the security of their liberties.

Throughout the Confederate States, we saw this great revolution effected without violence or suspension of the laws or the closing of the courts, the military power was nowhere placed above the civil authorities. None were seized and imprisoned at the mandate of arbitrary power. All division among the people disappeared, and the determination became unanimous that there should never again be any union with the Northern States. Almost as one man, all who were able to bear arms rushed to the defense of an invaded country, and nowhere has it been found necessary to compel men TO SERVE or to enlist mercenaries by the offer of extraordinary bounties.

But, in the Northern States, the Cherokee people saw with alarm a violated constitution, all civil liberty put in peril, and all rules of civilized warfare and the dictates of common humanity and decency unhesitatingly disregarded. In states which still adhered to the Union, a military despotism had displaced the civil power and the laws became silent amid arms. Free speech and almost free thought became a crime. The right of the writ of habeas corpus, guaranteed by the constitution, disappeared at the nod of a Secretary of State or a general of the lowest grade. The mandate of the Chief Justice of the Supreme Court was at naught by the military power, and this outrage on common right, approved by a President sworn to support the constitution. War on the largest scale was waged, and the immense bodies of troops called into the field in the absence of any law warranting it under the pretense of suppressing unlawful combination of men.

The humanities of war, which even barbarians respect, were no longer thought worthy to be observed. Foreign mercenaries and the scum of the cities and the inmates of prisons were enlisted and organized into brigades and sent into Southern States to aid in subjugating a people struggling for freedom, to burn, to plunder, and to commit the basest of outrages on the women. While the heels of armed tyranny trod upon the necks of Maryland and Missouri, and men of the highest character and position were incarcerated upon suspicion and without process of law, in jails, in forts, and prison ships, and even women were imprisoned by the arbitrary order of a President and Cabinet Ministers; while the press ceased to be free, and the publication of newspapers was suspended and their issues seized and destroyed. The officers and men taken prisoners in the battles were allowed to remain in captivity by the refusal of the Government to consent to an exchange of prisoners; as they had left their dead on more than one field of battle that had witnessed their defeat, to be buried and their wounded to be cared for by southern hands.

Whatever causes the Cherokee people may have had in the past to complain of some of the Southern states, they cannot but feel that their interests and destiny are inseparably connected with those of the south. The war now waging, is a war of Northern cupidity and fanaticism against the institution of African servitude; against the commercial freedom of the South, and against the political freedom of the states, and its objects are to annihilate the sovereignty of those states and utterly change the nature of the general government.

The Cherokee people and their neighbors were warned before the war commenced that the first object of the party which now holds the powers of government of the United States would be to annul the institution of slavery in the whole Indian country and make it what they term free territory and after a time a free state; and they have been also warned by the fate which has befallen those of their race in Kansas, Nebraska and Oregon that at no distant day they too would be compelled to surrender their country at the demand of Northern rapacity, and be content with an extinct nationality, and with reserves of limited extent for individuals, of which their people would soon be despoiled by speculators, if not plundered unscrupulously by the state.

Urged by these considerations, the .Cherokees, long divided in opinion. became unanimous, and like their brethren, the Creeks, Seminoles, Choctaws, and Chickasaws, determined, by the undivided voice of a General Convention of all the people, held at Tahlequah on the twenty-first day of August, in the present year, to make common cause with the South and share its fortunes.

In now, carrying this resolution into effect and consummating a treaty of alliance and friendship with the Confederate States of America, the Cherokee people declare that they have been faithful and loyal to their engagements with the United States until, by placing their safety and even their national existence in eminent peril, those States have released them from those engagements.

Menaced by a great danger, they exercise the inalienable right of self defense, and declare themselves a free people, independent of the Northern States of America, and at war with them by their own act. Obeying the dictates of prudence and providing for the general safety and welfare, confident of the rectitude of their intentions and true to the obligations of duty and honor, they accept the issue thus forced upon them, unite their fortunes now and forever with those of the Confederate States, and take up arms for the common cause, and with entire confidence in the justice of that cause and with a firm reliance upon Divine Providence, will resolutely abide the consequences."

JOSHUA ROSS,
Clerk National Committee.
THOMAS PEGG,

President of National Committee.
LACEY MOUSE,
Speaker of Council.
THOMAS B. WOLF,
Clerk of Council.
Approved. JOHN ROSS."

The failure of the United States government to give the protection guaranteed by the treaties with the Southern Indians was the real cause, according to some researchers, of their entering into an alliance with the Confederacy and was the primary cause of their allegiance staying with the South. If, at any time, during the first year of hostilities, the Federals could have shown themselves in absolute possession of Indian Country, the treaties with South would have dissolved. Success wins support everywhere at all times and under all circumstances.

With the Cherokee Nation now firmly allied with the South, Stand Watie, still an independent command, met with General McCulloch at Camp Walker, Benton County, Arkansas. He received a Colonel's commission and his unit designated the Cherokee Mounted Rifles. Watie and his men impressed the General so, that he wrote to Secretary Walker in September 1861:

"Watie's Regiment is composed of half-breeds, men generally educated and good soldiers in or out of the Nation. I hope the government will continue this gallant man and true friend of our country in service."

The time was approaching and would soon be here, when the United States government and all authority under it, would do well to remember where blame for the Indian defection really lay. Shirkers of responsibility have proverbially short memories. Close to 15,000 Indians fled the Nations and lived as exiles and outcasts in Kansas, solely because the United States government was not able to give them protection in their own homes.

Chief Ross appointed the following officers for Drew's Regiment; Colonel: John Drew, Lt. Col. William Potter Ross; Major: Thomas Pegg; Adjutant: James S. Vann; Surgeon: Dr. Robert D. Ross; Chaplain: Lewis Downing; Captains: Company A- Pickens M. Benge; Co. B-Richard Fields; Co. C-John Porum Davis; Co. D-James McDaniel; Co. E- Lewis Ross succeeded by Newton Hildebrand; Co.F- William W Albert; Co. G- Anderson Springston; Co. H. Nicholas Byers Sunders; Co. I- George M. Murrell; succeeded by Jefferson Hicks; Co. K- George Washington Scraper; Co. L James Vann.

Drew's Regiment consisted of 11 companies, each recruited in a separate district, Tahlequah, Saline, Canadian, Delaware, Flint, Illinois, Going Snake, Sequoyah, and Cooweescoowee. The enlisted men were full bloods and the officers were mixed bloods and affiliated with Ross's party. A good percentage of the officers were related to John Ross and his immediate family.

The officers tended to be educated men and had English names, but the full bloods went by their Indian names. Most Cherokee had English Christian names as well as their Cherokee names. Often their names were translated into English which could result in one person being called three sets of names, spellings varied according to the person's ability to read and write. This created confusion in written records and makes it difficult to locate information, especially on the full bloods.

Most of the enlisted men were members of the Keetoowah Society, a secret organization of full bloods founded by 2 abolitionist preachers, Evan Jones and his son, John Buttrick Jones. It formed in 1859 to preserve the religious and moral codes of the old Keetoowah Society which had been abandoned years before. These "pin Indians" as they were referred to, were politically opposed to Watie. The members wore peculiar crossed pins, sometimes of feathers, and believed in preserving Cherokee independence, tribal customs, and traditions. Some of the older Pins were among those who had assassinated members of the Treaty Party; among those were Watie's half brother, his uncle and cousin.

Watie's troops were designated the Second Regiment of Cherokee Mounted Rifles, while Col. Drew's was First Regiment of Cherokee Mounted Rifles. This undoubtedly irritated Watie, since his unit was the first organized and the unit organized by Ross would have this designation. The two units had a very uneasy spirit of cooperation between them. Confederate Creek Indians organized into the First Creek Cavalry Regiment led by their war chief, Col. Daniel McIntosh. His brother, Lt. Col. Chilly McIntosh, led a mixed unit of Creeks and Seminoles known as the First Seminole Cavalry Battalion with the Seminole Tribe's Confederate leader, Maj. John Jumper, second in command. Meanwhile Choctaw and Chickasaw warriors trained and organized into the First Regiment of Choctaw and Chickasaw Mounted Rifles under Col. Douglas Cooper.

Cooper was a white-bearded former U. S. Indian agent who, despite his fondness for liquor, was highly respected by the Choctaw Tribe, a people whom he honestly served before and after the war. A veteran of the Mexican War, he was the second ranking military officer in all Indian Territory. Overall command of Confederate Indian forces fell upon the shoulders of Albert Pike. Grateful for the success of his treaty mission, the Confederate government commissioned Pike a brigadier general and in November put him officially in charge of the Department of Indian Territory.

By October, Pike headed home with his collection of signed treaties. The different tribes and Nations having made treaties with the Confederate Government were: The Creek Nation, July 10, 1861; Choctaws and Chickasaws, July 12, 1861; Seminoles August 1, 1861; Shawnees, Delaware, Wichita, and affiliated tribes in the Leased Territory, August 12, 1861; The Comanches of the prairie, August 12, 1861; the Great Osages, October 2, 1861; the Senacas, and Shawnees (Neosho Agency) October 4, 1861; the Quapaws, October 4, 1861; the Cherokees, October 7, 1861.

The Confederacy had made some serious commitments to the tribes of Indian Territory. They had promised arms, provisions; pay and that the tribes would not be called to fight unless their Territory was invaded.

Chapter Three

Round Mountain

Before he left, word came to Pike of the unrest in Creek country and that a bloody uprising flamed in Creek country and threatened to engulf the entire Indian Nation. The old Creek chief, O-pothle-yaholo, violently opposed to the Confederate Alliances with the Five Nations, had gathered 2,000 of his warriors and gone on the warpath. Pike ordered Colonel Cooper to investigate.

Pike had sent a letter to O-pothle-yoholo stating the Confederate states offered a free pardon to him and all warriors under him in arms against the Confederate States and the Creek Nation, if they would lay down their arms. He offered that a battalion be organized under an officer of their choosing, which would be received into the Confederacy, and not marched beyond the limits of Indian Country without their permission.

The African Creeks and African Seminole, both Freemen and slaves, many with Creek and Seminole parentage as well as African, had considerable freedom before the War. They had considerable independence and for many years played a major roll in the social, cultural, and economic life of the Indian Nation. African Creek slaves and Freemen had enjoyed a degree of freedom unmatched in any of the slave states.

The pro–Southern Creeks looked at the scant supervision of the nearly two thousand African Creeks – as well as the nearly three hundred free blacks - as a threat to the slave system. They urged the Creek Council to put an end to this freedom. The council passed a series of new laws that were to take effect by March 1861. The provisions would confine slaves to their master's lands, institute a pass and patrol system, and forbid slaves to own livestock or other property or hire out their own labor for their own profit. The new laws also instructed the free blacks to re-enter slavery by selecting a master. The blacks were told to dispose of all their property before entering slavery. They had until March 10 to do this or they would be sold into slavery to the highest bidder. Tribal officers were appointed to oversee the free blacks' return to slavery, and the Creek Lighthorse, the tribal law enforcement body was given authority to enforce the new code.

When the pro-southern leaders of the Lower Towns signed treaties with the Confederacy, raised two Creek Confederate Regiments, in July 1861, they now had the power in the council to enforce these new laws. At a meeting August 5, O-pothle-yoholo, along with other Upper Creek leaders, refused the terms of the treaty.

O-pothle-yoholo now reached out to the Africans in the Creek and Seminole Nations. He sent agents into the black settlements of both Nations, promising freedom, if they would join the "Loyal Creeks." Here he found willing allies. Faced with the choice of complete slavery and a degree of freedom, they needed little persuasion.

They left their stores filled with merchandise, blacksmith shops, farms with crops, fruit trees, and abandoned the ranches with hay and fodder, bringing what livestock they could. Upper Creek masters provided their slaves with wagons, provisions, weapons, so that together they make the trek to the north.

Pro-Union refugees from the Seminole Nation, a Confederate ally, streamed to O-Pothle-yohola's camp at the Deep Fork of the Canadian River in western Creek Territory with their wagons and horses. The herds of these uninvited guests, said to be close to four thousand, including a thousand warriors, ate his grass.

Rumors were rampant in the camp, one being that the Confederate Indians were preparing to attack and massacre the Union leaders. Another, that Jim Lane's Kansas troops were on their way to reinforce the Union Indians, so they could drive the rebels out of the Territory.

The old chief, believing the first rumor, dumped the Creek Treasury into a barrel and buried it in the hills. He ordered his people to leave, saying he was going to the western lands to set up cow pens. The debates still go on as to what was really in the old chief's mind. Watie felt the Creeks and their refugees would circle to Kansas for protection and would be a problem in the future.

A Confederate Creek scouting report informed Colonel McIntosh that a party of O-Pothle-yohola's followers that included "a large lot of Negroes" had crossed the Deep Fork River and were moving west and to the north. McIntosh and the other Indian officers decided it was time to act swiftly. They told Colonel Cooper that they intended to move against O-Pothle-yohola and his party and that, "all free Negroes found with Hopothleyahola's party and taken during the expedition shall be sold as slaves for the benefit of the Nation. All slaves taken in this expedition who have runaway from their owners who are residents of another Nation shall be dealt with according to Creek law."

Major John Jumper's Confederate Seminoles were eager to battle the Creeks under Alligator and Billy Bowlegs. Chilly and Daniel McIntosh rallied the Creeks, because of O-Pothle-yohola's seizure of the treasury. Cooper countermanded their retaliatory threat.

Cooper's expedition moved against the Loyal Muskogees on November 4. Confederate Indian troops, along with Texans, followed. As they moved north, the land had grown rugged and broken, with gullies and draws filled with brush and timber. Travel was difficult for the wagons as they bumped and rocked over the uneven ground. It was a country made by the gods for ambush and war. Half the land they moved over was prairie, the other covered with oak and hickory, providing some protection. As they moved slowly north, there were signs others had come this way, but were they friends or foes? Then came charred cabins and burned fields. Sometimes at night, they could see an eerie orange glow in the sky, as another place burned.

The Confederates, numbering over 1,000, set out from Fort Gibson for Creek country through the warm fall weather. Just looking at the scenery, one would not suspect what was to come. The browns, golds and reds of the trees, and the warm sun, belied the black specter that was still closing in on the Territory. Although the soldiers could feel it down deep, this day made it seem far away and not so imminent.

Cooper found the situation worse then he thought. He rode into Creek country with a small escort and found the camp on the old chief's land near North Fork Town on the Canadian River. O-pothle-yoholo had more than 3,500 Indians, many women and children, but also a fighting force of about 1,500 warriors. Most were Creek, but a few Seminole, including the Seminole war captains, Alligator, Holata Micco and Halleck Tustenuggee, armed with muzzle-loading shotguns, hunting rifles, knives, tomahawks, bow and arrow, spears and war clubs. Also in this group were a number of former slaves, who had escaped and fled to O-pothle-yohola's camp where they were welcomed and armed as fighting men.

Cooper's informants said that O-pothle-yohola had been in contact with E. H. Curruth, a US Indian

Agent in Kansas, who was encouraging the old chief to continue resisting the Confederates that the US Army would soon be in Indian Territory.

Cooper had been unable to reconcile differences with O-pothle-yohola, who commanded Union forces of Creek and Seminole. He was hoping to divert a war flaring within the Nations. The old chief refused to even dignify Cooper's written requests with an answer. So, he returned to Fort Gibson for reinforcements and supplies. Because of the large herd of livestock the Creeks had, they moved their camp, in the meantime, to find better grazing for their stock, and headed northwest to be closer to Kansas.

The large number of wagons meant they could not all travel together and the stock would starve for lack of grass if not broken into smaller herds. They would all have to move in parallel columns and several days apart. Any of the wagon trains could be overwhelmed if overtaken, but it was the only way. Once the wagons and stock were on their way, the warriors would follow riding between the families and the enemy. A smaller group would race ahead to secure crossings on the Arkansas. With any luck, the Union would be waiting for them. The morning the first wagons left was gray and misting, the kind of mist that soaks to the skin, wagon wheels soon caked with red clay which had to be removed constantly. O-pothle-yoholo was with the last group to leave. More joined as the wagons moved north. At Tiger Town, it was the Yuchis - Children of the Sun, then the Alabamas, The Alabamas were as ancient as the land and the rivers. They had the memories of animals from the time of the deep cold, the ones with the long tusks and trunks and the man killer cats with sharp teeth. From the west came the Delaware and Shawnees, the Quapaw, Kickapoo and Piankashaw, Wichita, and the Kadohadachos. They came by wagon and on foot, pinning their fate to the old ways and the old gods. Finally, from the east came Cherokee in spite of John Ross and Stand Watie.

The early November warmth had chilled as Cooper set out from North Fork Town, on November 15 with 1, 400 troops, six companies of the First Choctaw and Chickasaws Mounted Rifles, First Creek Cavalry, under Colonel Daniel N. McIntosh, First Seminole Cavalry Battalion, under Lt. Colonel Chilly McIntosh and Major John Jumper, the Seminole. There were 500 troopers of the Ninth Texas under Lt. Colonel William Quayle, of Johnson Station, Tarrant County, Texas, which included the companies of Captains M. J. Brimson, Tarrant County, J. E. McCool, Grayson County, and Charles S. Stewart of Titus County. They were to either force submission or drive him from the country. He was sure he would catch up with them, as the chief had women and children with their baggage wagons and livestock and the weather was getting colder.

The Texas Cavalry reached Boggy Depot on November 5 and rested a few days, foraging, replenishing their supplies, and then proceeded to North Fork Town on the 11th. On the 12th, Quayle's Cavalry pushed northwest, riding 65 miles, by 10:00 PM to join Cooper's forces.

O-pothle-yohola had organized his forces near the North Fork of the Canadian River, a few miles north of Greenleaf Town. He believed at least half of the Creek Nation was behind him, and that the Confederate forces were going to attack. He thought he could hold his own with the enemy and withdraw gradually toward Kansas and the protection of the Union guns.

When they camped that night, they knew they were still a day or two away from the Arkansas. Nevertheless, there was another delay. From the west, a dark cloud rolled in, with wind and rain. The sharp, chilling wind blew in heavy gusts, with thunder and lightening. The cold rain swallowed everything as it moved across the prairie. The people huddled under the wagons and carts hoping to stay dry, but it was of no use. Puddles formed and every ditch and draw was soon rushing water. As quick as it had moved in, the storm moved on, the sun came out and the dark clouds moved on toward the Kiamichi Mountains, but the cold wind remained.

They could not move on the next day because of high water. By night, the puddles had disappeared, but the air grew colder and by morning, there was ice on the puddles and frost covered the ground. The wagons again moved out, heading for the Arkansas.

Cooper rode up the Deep Fork of the Canadian River toward O-pothle-yohola's camp, which he found deserted. Sighting some campfire smoke in the distance, Cooper sent Col. Quayle's Texans to charge the camp. They found this camp also deserted. Quayle decided this camp was only an outpost and spotting a group of Creek scouts and smoke in the distance, followed them back to camp. The Texans chased them across the prairie until dark to an area called Round Mountain, actually a small hill or mound, near the present town of Keystone in the northern Creek country.

It was not a very impressive landmark except that it overlooked the first real test of arms of the Civil War in Indian Territory.

After the families had moved on to the Arkansas, O-pothle-yoholo stayed behind with a small army of warriors from nearly twenty Nations. They took a different path heading to the northwest. They would leave a deliberate trail with abandoned buggies and wagons, camp litter, and lame ponies. It was an old trick, but had worked before. By sunrise, O-pothle-yoholo was nearing a low range of hills rolling off to the east. Away from the hills, setting like a haystack was a small rounded hill. The country was mostly prairie, with small clusters of cedars and scrub oak near the ravines and gullies, coarse grass and flint ridges, colored gold by the season and the morning sun.

The warriors painted for war, their faces half red for war and half black for death. Some removed their shirts and painted their bodies with colors of war and death. All of them had cornhusks in their hair, a symbol of loyalty to the old chief, and feathers. They rode with weapons ready, hoping the enemy would follow them and not the families.

At a tree-lined ravine, the Chief stopped them. He ordered billowing fires be built to attract the enemy then placed his men along the ravine. It ran from the direction they had come like a large bow. Soon every bush, tree, and rock had a warrior behind it. They waited for the enemy to come to them.

Quayle had found the camp, and the old chief was waiting for him. As the troopers followed them in, a hail of bullets from the concealed Warriors fell on the stunned Texans, from a line of trees along the banks of a small creek. The Creeks sent a rider less horse chased by dogs through the melee adding more confusion as bullets hit riders and screaming horses. The Texans had not noticed the trees that concealed the Creeks were horseshoe shaped and they were in a trap from three sides. Adding to the confusion, the Creeks had set fire to the prairie behind the Texans, which highlighted their targets. Both rifle fire and arrows rained on the Cavalry. In confusion, the Texans made a hasty retreat, with the Creek warriors following. Cooper heard the gunfire, and quickly moved to meet Quayle. Colonel McIntosh's Creek Regiment came up to assist the Texans, but found themselves covering their retreat, firing, and then falling back.

The old chief soon realized his position was not good. Unlike Cooper's force, his men had never received any regular military training, while Cooper's combined units of well-drilled Texas Cavalry and trained Indian troops presented a formidable force. As a diversion to cover their retreat, a group of Union Indians slipped around and started a prairie fire beyond the right flank of the Confederates, threatening their supply wagons. Colonel Cooper chose not to pursue them in the darkness, to avoid more confusion

Company K of the Choctaw-Chickasaw Regiment under Captain R. A. Young had moved up and dismounted to the left of the Texans, the main body of the Choctaw-Chickasaw Regiment under Captains Welch, Hall, Reynolds, and McCurtain had moved up and was taking fire. Now it was so dark, that it was difficult to separate friend and foe. Because of darkness, Cooper did not order the troops to fire until they were within 60 yards. Pulling back, a scouting party of about 50 men rode out to find the Union Indians had left the field. O-Pothle-yohola's warriors had done their job well, stopping Cooper and causing the loss of men and horses.

O-pothle-yoholo, his enemy stopped briefly, ordered a night withdrawal north toward Kansas. The women took a firm grip on their hominy pestles and approached the prisoners taken in the fighting. These captives, tied hand and foot, knew what fate awaited them.

Arriving at the Creek abandoned camp the next morning, the Rebels found a few sheep and oxen, several old horses, and some broken wagons, as well as some sacks of coffee, sugar, and other foodstuffs scattered around. The Creek chief's people had escaped with most of their livestock and other possessions. Cooper reported his casualties in the skirmish at Round Mountain (Battle of Red Forks) as six killed, four wounded and one missing. There is no record of O-pothle-yohola's losses. Round Mountain was the first serious clash in Indian Territory.

Breaking off from their foes, O-pothle-yohola's warriors joined their families already fleeing northeast. Crossing the cold Arkansas River during the night, they left the Creek Nation and crossed into the Cherokee Nation heading for a village of Union sympathizing Cherokee on Bird Creek.

Bird Creek (Chusto-Talasah)

Colonel Cooper received orders from General McCulloch to break off his pursuit of the old Creek and march east to the Arkansas border where McCulloch was mustering all the troops he could to stand off an advancing Union army of 20,000 under the command of Major General John C. Fremont. After 4 days March, Cooper received another communiqué from McCulloch that the Union forces were returning north, so he was free to continue his pursuit of O-pothle-yohola. Word also reached Cooper that O-pothle-yohola had not continued his withdrawal to Kansas, but had camped in the southeast corner of the Cherokee Nation at Chusto-Talasah on Bird Creek at a place called High Shoals by the white men.

It was the end of the timber and brush as the Loyal Indians knew it. Ahead was plains country, open, rolling, and endless, with the cold wind still blowing, nothing to block it from the people camped there. Some of the younger men had never seen the plains. Without trees and mountains, where would the owls nest, and what would shield the earth from the cold? It was the end of the earth.

The people camped in the timber by the Arkansas River and nearby streams. With the many Nations camped there, soon problems arose. Some

Kickapoo stole horses from the Yuchis. The Alabamas would not camp near the Wichitas. The fierce pride that made many of the Nations and peoples courageous, able to withstand almost anything, divided them also, one against the other. There was also mounting trouble between the miccos and leaders of the towns and other Nations. It was not their way to follow blindly. Some talked about digging in and waiting for the soldiers from the North. Some thought they should continue before rains turned to sleet and snow. Some argued that the white men from the North were not riding in to meet them, but were waiting in Kansas. Still others hitched up their wagons to leave, not for Kansas, but for home. The battle at Round Mountain had been the war. Never in their wildest dreams did they believe what was coming!

On November 29, Cooper's forces left camp at Spring Hill near Concharta on the Arkansas River, well fed, rested and ready for action. He moved his troopers out in two columns to catch the Creeks in the middle. He led one column of Indian Troops, about 800 men of the Choctaw-Chickasaw Mounted Rifles, the Choctaw Battalion, and the First Creek Regiment, following a road northwest toward Tulsey Town (now the city of Tulsa) where his scouts said the Union Indians were camped. One of Cooper's Indian scouts was a young mixed blood Cherokee rifleman, named Clem Vann Rogers, who would become a Captain under Stand Watie and who's son Will, was destined to be the world famous entertainer and humorist, Will Rogers

The second column consisted of the Ninth Texas Cavalry under Colonel William B. Sims, and Lt. Colonel Quayle. Sims's orders were to join the First Cherokee Mounted Rifles of Colonel John Drew near a village called Coody's Bluff, (just west of Nowata, in Nowata County) on the Verdigris River.

When Cooper camped near Tulsey Town, he had a chance to talk to a Confederate who had been a prisoner in O-pothle-yohola's camp on Bird Creek and had escaped. He described the location of the Union Indians' camp and told Cooper he had about 2,000 warriors and planned to attack Cooper's army soon. Cooper sent staff officers to contact Sims and Drew. Because of the confusion in orders, Drew's Regiment marched to a point on Bird Creek, while Sims' Texans joined Cooper at the new rendezvous point. Unfortunately, this placed Drew's 480 Confederate troops only about 6 miles northeast of O-pothle-yohola's camp with 2,000 Union warriors, and reinforcements more than 24 hours away.

The chief had deployed his warriors among the trees and rocks, and built large billowing fires to attract an enemy. Then they waited. O-pothle-yohola knew the enemy was near, even before the scouts spoke, he could feel their presence. In the distance, an owl hooted four times. Overhead, a single star glistened in a red orange western sky, the star of death. The late November weather was getting colder. The farther north they traveled meant less protection from the elements. The trees and cover were beginning to thin as the plains of Kansas drew closer.

Drew posted a series of strong outposts to guard against a surprise attack, dug in and nervously waited for Cooper and Sims. If the Creek and Seminole warriors decided to attack, they would easily over run his forces. Most of the full bloods were opposed to making war on O-pothle-yohola's people, and were still uneasy after Cooper and Sims arrived and camped about two miles from Drew. He informed Cooper that O-pothle-yoholo had sent word expressing a desire for peace. With Cooper's blessing, Drew sent his second in command, Major Pegg to meet the Creek Chief. Pegg returned with word that he had not been able to talk to

O-pothle-yoholo, saying several thousand warriors in full war paint surrounded him. The meeting was a ruse. Everywhere there were warriors streaked in paint, roaring campfires, the sounds of drums and war chants and huge numbers of men waving weapons. O-pothle-yoholo was nowhere in sight.

With the Confederate delegation surrounded, the Keetoowah in Colonel Draw's regiment made their move. Unknown to Drew, for months they had been planning a way to destroy Confederate power in the Cherokee Nation; as had O-pothle-yoholo, ever since John Ross had betrayed him and joined the South. For days, O-pothle-yoholo and the Keetoowah had been in contact. That night the Keetoowah spread the rumor of Drew's Regiment being attacked and overwhelmed; the only way to survive was to join O-pothle-yohola or die. O-pothle-yoholo had powers and magic that his enemies had never imagined, no one could stand against him.

The Cherokee Regiment panicked at hearing the news. News of the war paint had the desired effect on Drew's command. His Cherokee refused to attack the full bloods and withdrew from the battle. Colonel Drew failed to recognize the possible situation in the grumbling of his troops against this Confederate pursuit of the old chief.

On the night before the battle, December 8, Col. Drew walked out of his warm, heated tent into the cold night air and suddenly became aware of how quiet it was around him. The usual camp noises were gone, the low hum of voices, the occasional snort from the horses on the picket line. It was much too silent for an armed camp of over 400 men and equipment. Nearly all his men had deserted, slipping away in the darkness, taking their horses and weapons with them. Shaken, Drew called his orderly, who was still there, to saddle and bring his horse to him. Arousing the few men left, about 60, he headed for Cooper's camp. He then realized he had left his supply of ammunition behind. Sending a few men on to tell Cooper, he returned to retrieve the wagon before it fell into enemy hands.

With a well planned assault and thousands of attackers Cooper surrounded Yohola, and revenge for Round Mountain was at hand. However, Cooper had not counted on Drew's insincerity. When word reached Cooper, he angrily ordered his drummer to beat the "long roll" a call to formation under arms. He sent troops to cover all approaches to the camp, and sent Colonel Quayle with a squadron of Texans to the abandoned camp. The next morning, December 9, Cooper ordered Drew to take his remaining Cherokee and a detachment of Texans and Choctaw to retrieve whatever remained at the camp. Cooper no doubt wished that Stand Watie and his loyal Confederate troops were along instead of Drew's rebellious troops, but Watie's Second Cherokee Mounted Rifles were still on duty at old Fort Wayne near the Arkansas border. When Drew returned with his equipment and horses, Cooper broke camp.

The Rebels were ready for a fight, but anxious, too. What had happened the night before was unnerving; an entire regiment - troops they had counted on - had simply vanished. More anxious than any, was probably Daniel McIntosh. All his life, he had seen O-pothle-yoholo manipulate others with words. When he was a child, O-Pothle-yohola's men had murdered his father and other family members in the old country; his ancestors screamed for revenge.

In the old days in Alabama, O-pothle-yoholo should have been put to death for pushing the sale of tribal lands to the Federal government; then signing the treaty to make it happen. Nevertheless, he was able to walk away from the council free. Those who condemned the McIntosh as traitors never seemed to remember that O-pothle-yoholo had signed the treaty giving away millions of acres to the United States, that he was guilty as anyone of handing over the ancient lands to the white man. They seemed to forget as well, that the lands he signed away belonged to only the people of the Lower towns, people like the McIntosh! O-pothle-yoholo had organized the Upper towns, challenged the authority and position of the McIntosh for his own ends. He was behind resistance to the Confederacy, visiting every town and farm, whipping up bitterness, dredging up old hatreds and ripping apart Indian Territory. As he rode, Daniel McIntosh swore on the memory of his father, he would put an end to O-pothle-yoholo.

Cooper left his train under the guard of 100 men, sent out two companies of the Creek Regiment under Captain Foster to find the Union Indians, and formed his troops into three columns. He sent the Choctaw-Chickasaw Regiment to the right, put the rest of Drew's Cherokees and the Texans in the center and sent the Creeks to the left. Foster did his job well, soon riding in chased by the Loyal Creeks, with six prisoners. Cooper could see the Union pickets at various points in the timber along Bird Creek. Information was that O-Pothle-yohola's forces were further down the creek.

By afternoon, advance Confederate scouts were skirmishing with the Union Indians along Bird Creek. Suddenly there was heavy gunfire at the rear of the Confederate column. Cooper's force turned to meet the attack, not realizing it was part of O-pothle-yohola's plan to draw them to his chosen battle site. He had sent 200 warriors to attack and then retreat to his position, drawing the Confederates into a trap. The rear guard was in immediate peril and would have been cut up badly, had not Captain Young, in charge of the Choctaw-Chickasaw squadron in the rear, seen the danger, whirled his troops and charged the Creeks.

The Union warriors were strongly posted along a gorge at a bend in Bird Creek, called Chusto-Talasah. A large number of Drew's Cherokee deserters, who had taken their weapons along, had joined the Union Creeks, Seminoles, and slaves.

Captains Jones and McCurtain swung their Choctaw-Chickasaw companies to the right, joining Young, and Colonel D. N. McIntosh's Confederate Creeks swung left, closing with the enemy on the creek. Jones and McCurtain advanced rapidly across the prairie to about 100 yards, then dismounted and advanced, firing as they ran.

In the meantime, the Texans and other Choctaw-Chickasaw units, driving the loyal Creeks across the prairie toward the creek, were attacking O-Pothle-yohola's forces on the prairie. Quayle charged with his detachment and drove the Union back toward the timberline. McIntosh's Confederate Creeks on the left shrieked and yelled as they closed with the enemy and met their Northern Creek brothers in hand to hand combat. Their action was probably the best for the day, as they successfully pushed their opponents back deep into the horseshoe bend.

The battle wore on for four hours. The amount of gunpowder expended resulted in very limited casualties. Fighting Indian fashion, from behind cover, it was like a turkey shoot with hundreds of heads popping in and out of view for a split second. Late in the day, a group of Union Indians, in war paint, made a dash for the Choctaw-Chickasaw Regiments horses, which in typical Cavalry fashion, one in four Cavalrymen held when they dismounted to fight. Colonel Cooper sent a detachment of cavalry to assist the horse holders. The charge failed, but when word spread of the charge on the horses, most of the Choctaw and Chickasaw troopers abandoned their positions and ran for their horses. Losing his horse in a fight like this and stranded on enemy grounds could cost a man his life. Major Michael LeFlore desperately tried to rally the disorganized Indians, but the sun was setting before they redeployed. As the fighting faded in the darkness, Col. Cooper recalled his troops, retired from the battle field and camped for the night about 5 miles away.

The warriors disappeared through the woods and across the creek into the night. Nothing remained, but the sounds of the wounded and a rising northeast wind. Low, heavy clouds brought the first snow of the season. The snow soon went away, but the rain that followed was a slow constant, soaking drizzle, turning campsites into mud and every road into a pond or stream.

The next morning Cooper sent a strong detail to check the enemy positions and found the O-Pothle-yohola had abandoned the camp during the night. Their trails led to the northeast. The weather had turned decidedly cold and snow had begun to fall on the Cherokee Nation. Cooper set a burial detail to take care of the dead on the battlefield. Confederate casualties were 15 dead, 37 wounded, and of course, no record for O-pothle-yohola, but Cooper estimated about 500 dead and wounded. More likely, O-Pothle-yohola's loses were about the same as Cooper's, who had put the best face he could on his official report to the Secretary of War.

The large amount of gunfire at Bird Creek had exhausted the munitions supply so the Confederates had to return to Fort Gibson for more supplies. Worried that the desertion of Drew's men would lead to more desertions and perhaps a shift on loyalties in Indian Territory, Cooper sent to the Confederate high command in Arkansas for reinforcements.

The Creeks had enough powder for maybe one more battle. There would be no supplies or ammunition unless they came from Kansas and every bullet would have to be made and dram of powder count. Their wagons could not move through the mud, laden with everything they owned. The cattle and horses stripped the country of grass, became weak and many were turned out onto open range, lost to their owners. The rains let up and the wagons began moving again. Then the rain came again, the cold slow drizzle.

Arriving at Choska in Creek territory, Cooper left the main body of his men there and rode on 20 miles to Fort Gibson. Waiting for him was a message from Colonel James McIntosh in Van Buren.

McCulloch had gone to Richmond, and a young West Point graduate, Colonel James McIntosh (no relation to the Creek officers) was in charge. The young Colonel agreed there was need for concern and being a man of action, took to the field himself leading a Confederate force of 1,600 of his best horsemen, all veterans of Wilson's Creek, and rode to join Cooper at Fort Gibson, southwest of Tahlequah. These troops arrived at Fort Gibson on December 20. There the two men planned a trap for O-pothle-yoholo.

At the end of one long weary day, scouts rode in with word for O-pothle-yoholo; Stand Watie's Cherokee in the east were on the move. There were no Keetoowah with Watie, his men were loyal to the South, and the Keetoowah were their blood enemies. Stand Watie's troops would come as one against the Creeks. Scouts reported a fresh column of Confederates riding out of Arkansas, heavily armed and larger than the Creeks had seen before. These forces, along with troops under Cooper and the McIntosh would far outnumber the Creeks. If they all attacked together, the Creeks would be overwhelmed.

The enemy would not be tricked with another ambush. If they stayed and fought, they would be overwhelmed. If they scattered, they would be hunted down and killed. There was only one chance; some would die so others could live. The warriors would have to stand their ground fighting to the death, buying time with their lives so the rest could flee. The outcome was certain for the outnumbered and hopelessly outgunned warriors.

Chustenalah/Caving Banks (Shoal Creek)

On December 22, Colonel James McIntosh left Fort Gibson with 5 companies of Lt. Colonel Walter P. Lane's 3rd Texas Cavalry Regiment, Lt. Colonel John S. Griffith's 6th Cavalry, 7 companies of Colonel W. C. Young's 11th Texas, 4 companies of Colonel McIntosh's 2nd Arkansas Mounted Rifles and Captain H. S. Bennett's Lamar Texas Cavalry Company, 1,380 men. According to latest information, O-pothle-yohola's camp was located on Shoal Creek a tributary of the Verdigris River. The weather had turned miserably cold. A bitter wind swept through the hills and the camp, a howling mournful wind that came with clouds.

McIntosh would approach the Union Indians from the front, moving up the Verdigris with parts of the Third, Sixth, and 11th Texas Cavalry and Second Arkansas Mounted Rifles. Cooper, reinforced by John W. Whitfield's Texas Battalion would ride up the North side of the Arkansas and get in the rear. McIntosh picked up the old Chief's trail on December 25, following it into the Big Bend of the Arkansas; enemy snipers fired on his scouts as they forded Shoal Creek. McIntosh led a pursuit of the warriors, but soon concluded they were on a fruitless chase and ordered his men back to camp. This officer was too smart to fall for the same tricks used at Round Mountain and Bird Creek. O-pothle-yohola faced a force he had never seen before, this officer was a well-trained military man, and his men were real soldiers. They were tough frontier horsemen trained as a regular cavalry unit. Many were battle-hardened veterans of Wilson's Creek. They spent this bleak cold Christmas evening squaring away their gear and getting their weapons ready for battle.

During the night, a messenger from Cooper arrived with word that his progress up the Arkansas had been delayed because of desertion of a large number of his teamsters. Cooper figured it would be two or three days before he could be in position to support McIntosh. After reading the dispatch, McIntosh decided he would continue without Cooper. He would like to have his troops, but he felt their presence was not necessary for a victory. His cavalry regulars could take on the Union Indians. Suddenly the war in Indian Territory had taken on the appearance of the classic confrontation of White Cavalry and Indian Warriors.

The morning of December 26, 1861 was bitterly cold. Colonel McIntosh's cavalry rode steadily west toward Shoal Creek and the area known as Patriot Hills or Chustenahlah. They were careful in their approach, with scouts out in all directions watching for the enemy. O-pothle-yohola's scouts were also watching and by noon, the warriors were crouched behind a heavy growth of Blackjack trees on a steep rocky hill overlooking the creek. The Seminole War Chief, Halek Tustenuggee, had placed his troops along the slopes, under excellent cover and a good view of the creek.

As the first of McIntosh's troopers splashed across the cold, icy creek, the Union Indians opened fire from above them. The Texans dismounted, ran for cover, and returned fire. McIntosh dismounted his veterans and formed a line about 300 yards away from the Indians posted on top of a ridge overlooking Shoal Creek. After firing several volleys, the Confederates charged across an open field, splashed through the creek, and wormed their way up the rocky slope of the ridge only to be stopped and pinned down near the top by murderous fire from the Indians. They could not move for 2 hours, and then with the brassy call of the bugles, in a furious assault, LT. Colonel Walter P. Lane's 'screaming' Texans swept over the top and the battle of Chustenahlah was won. Suddenly, the Creeks found themselves running for their lives, relentlessly pursued by the Texans over five or six other ridges. Three times the warriors tried to make a stand, taking cover behind boulders, only to be crushed by the raging Texans. Three miles from the battle site, they gathered to make a last stand. Once more, the cavalry crushed their hopes. Until about sunset, when the bugles sounded recall, fleeing tribesmen were chased across the land and shot in their tracks.

Colonel McIntosh reported his casualties as 3 dead and 32 wounded. He estimated O-pothle-yohola's group killed as about 250. The Confederates captured 160 women and children, 20 blacks, 30 wagons, 70 yoke of oxen, about 500 horses, several cattle, 100 sheep, and thousands of dogs. No warriors were listed as captured. In the abandoned camp, the soldiers found hundreds of buffalo robes, and great quantities of food. The cavalrymen kept many beads and trinkets. One Texan found a very notable souvenir, a silver medal dated 1694, commemorating a peace treaty between the Creek Tribe and the British Government.

O-Pothle-yohola gathered the survivors and set out immediately for Kansas, his people forced to abandon much of what they needed for survival. The cold, sleet and snow, and the inevitable wind of the plains bore down on them as they struggled northward. The cold wind cuts clear to the bones in one of those winters in Oklahoma, and many would not make it to Kansas.

The people struggled on north all night, through the snow and cutting winds. Large numbers were scattered across the land with nothing, no wagons, no stock or food, nothing but the clothes and blankets on their backs. Among the survivors, the old chief was very ill, sick with fever and dread.

While in camp on Shoal Creek on December 27, McIntosh decided he had accomplished his mission. With O-pothle-yohola's rebellion crushed; he was no longer a threat to the Confederacy. His people scattered across the countryside, struggling through the sleet and snow toward Kansas. The long, cold trek ahead would be worse than anything they had faced up to that point.

At sundown, Colonel Stand Waite and his 300 Cherokee rode into camp and planned following the fugitives the next day. Colonel Cooper, still trying to catch up with McIntosh had sent orders to Watie on December 23, to rendezvous with McIntosh's cavalry as soon as possible. Dismounting, Watie's men could hardly believe what had happened. In a four-hour battle, the Texans had routed O-pothle-yohola, capturing several hundred men and women, a handful of Negroes, 39 wagons, 70 yoke of oxen, and over 500 ponies, while suffering only 9 killed and 40 wounded.

McIntosh was ready to head back to Arkansas, but Watie's arrival changed his mind. Why shouldn't they pursue the tired and dispirited Indians? Watie's men were anxious to get into the action, and why not use that enthusiasm to his advantage. He broke camp at dawn on the 27th. Watie's Cherokee, followed by Cooper's Choctaw and Chickasaw, spear headed the column in search of the Union Indian survivors, on that cold December 27. The Cherokee scouts under Captain Coody, soon found O-Pothle-yohola's trail and followed it about 25 miles, when they spotted a couple of wagons. To prevent their capture, the drivers cut the teams loose and set fire to the wagons. Watie located a sizable force and after a quick survey of their position, sent a message back to McIntosh, The tough little

Cherokee Colonel divided his force, sending half his force under Major Elias Boudinot with Captains Mayes, Parks, Bell, and Coody, to the left. He led the rest against the right of the Union Indians who had taken a position in a series of gorges. It was rough terrain, defended by desperate warriors, but after about an hour and half of grinding battle, the exhausted Creeks and Seminoles abandoned their defenses and continued to retreat. Boudinot's forces came upon a deep ravine used as a Union-hiding place, attacked and drove the enemy out, killing 15 Northern Indians and taking a number of women and children captive. The Union Creek and Seminoles were completely routed and at the mercy of Watie's merciless pursuit. In this almost forgotten, unnamed skirmish, there were 11 Union dead, none for Watie's troops and they captured about 75 women and children and 30 packhorses. With almost no food or supplies left, the northern Indians killed and ate their horses. Using the hides for shelter, with the freezing weather added to the fugitives' plight, some became so discouraged at the possibility of reaching Kansas they gave up.

As the day passed, it was colder and the snow was growing worse. Pushed by winds, it came down in lateral sheets, cutting visibility to a few feet. In the gullies and ravines, it deepened in drifts up to their waists, then as high as a man. The Cherokee and the Texans, nearly as miserable as those they chased, struggled through a frozen world of swirling white.

Then a change began. The animals first sensed it, the deer and small animals buried deeper into the snow along the creeks and hills. The air grew heavy and thick and from the northeast a bit of wind, cold and wet, began move the icy tree limbs and branches, causing them to snap. In swept the dark, fast moving clouds, blotting out the sun as an avenging spirit. Sleet started to fall and the winds moaned as another blizzard came roaring off the plains.

Chapter Four

1862

January 1 brought a fresh blanket of sleet and snow with winds as bitter as the first storm. It enabled the Confederates to follow several fleeing bands of Indians. Their trails generally led toward Walnut Creek in Kansas. The fleeing Union Indians with supplies gone and hope of reaching Kansas fast disappearing, watched the approaching horsemen, wondering if they would be the blue-coated cavalry sent to their rescue by Lane, hoping it would not be the hard riding Cherokee Rifles led by Stand Watie. When it turned out to be the dreaded Confederate Indians, the frightened mothers, even those that had bashed in the heads of their prisoners some hours ago, threw their babies into mud holes and stomped them to death rather than let them fall into the hands of the mixed bloods. However, Watie and Cooper were not making war on women and children, and none that surrendered harmed.

While Watie rode north, capturing stragglers and cornering Alligator, one of O-pothle-yohola's Seminole officers "Surrender or die" was the ultimatum given him. The Seminole took his choice- he died. Cooper and his Indians traveled northwest, following fresh tracks in the snow, searching clumps of trees and shrubbery, captured, and killed small bands of refugees hidden in makeshift shelters. At Fort Leavenworth, a Federal agent wired Washington that "O-pothle-yohola needs help badly." As thoroughly as possible, the Rebel leaders sought out the loyal bands, some hiding in brush shelters and some, having eaten their horses, hidden in hides.

Cooper's Indian troops and Texas cavalry hounded the miserable Indians. None of his troops was battle casualties, but the weather was so bitter and cold one Confederate trooper froze to death. This ended the Creek uprising in Indian Territory, as the freezing survivors crossed the border into Kansas. Freezing weather and disease continued to claim Indian lives as they huddled in refugee camps, praying for an early spring and swift revenge on the Confederates. About 700 of the fleeing Indians died, either because of the weather or under the Rebel guns. O-pothle-yohola reached safety at Leroy, Kansas. In the distance, looking north as far as the eye could see was a vast frozen plain, open and endless - nothing more. There were no forts or settlements, no farms, no fires, no waiting tents, no blankets, or food; there was nothing... It had all been a lie: the promises of support and troops, and the promise of supplies. It was another white man's lie. There was only a wasteland locked in ice, without a sign of life or hope.

Nearly nine thousand people from more than twenty nations fled north with O-pothle-yohola in the winter of 1861 - 1862. Possibly six thousand finally made it into Kansas, the rest were dead in the frozen mud and bloody ice of Indian Territory. In Kansas, their misery was not over. Over the next four years, many more died. Put into camps called Federal Compounds and security centers as well as reservations, they died by the hundreds from disease, exposure and starvation.

Frostbite, hunger, and disease were rampant. One of the first doctors on the scene, US Army Surgeon A. B. Campbell, reported over one hundred amputations in a few days. Campbell also said pneumonia, consumption, and other inflammatory diseases of the chest; throat and eyes associated with exposure were common among the refugees. Few had provisions for even the crudest of shelters and slept on the frozen ground with piles of prairie grass for bedding. Shoes were unknown and food and clothing were in short supply. Refugees wandered the camps, naked in the freezing temperatures, searching for food and clothing for them and their families.

The state of Kansas that bounded the northern line of the Cherokee Nation had just passed through a terrible drought in 1860. It paralyzed the business of the people, causing thousands to leave, discouraged. Those that remained were in no condition to help the Indians, because they were receiving food, clothing and help from the north. Their situation was desperate from the long drought. The few inches of rain that fell during the entire year broke all known records for rain in that region.

Cooper's troops turned back toward camp, reaching Tulsey Town on January 4, 1862, where a Confederate supply train was waiting, with food and supplies. Because Colonel Watie was in the forefront of this chase across Indian Territory, he became the hero of this wintry chase and Confederate newspapers erroneously reported he captured and burned Fort Scott, Topeka, and Lawrence. He was the hero of the Cherokee Nation.

While on the way back to Grand River with 800-900 head of cattle and 250 ponies captured from the Creeks, two companies of Watie's Regiment were sent to arrest a company of 50-60 armed pro-Union Cherokee nearby. These Loyal Cherokees had two wagons and were heading north to Kansas. In the ensuing fight, Watie's men killed one, captured seven, and scattered the rest. Once again, Colonel Watie's men showed they were not afraid to kill fellow Cherokees who sided with the Union. In fact, they seemed to relish the revenge.

The desertion of many of Drew's Cherokees to the Union during and shortly after the battle with O-pothle-yohola's Creeks, on Shoal Creek, caused the Confederate white troops to doubt future performance of the Indians. One Texan wrote, "I do not like to fight with Indians very much, for you do not know at what moment they will turn over to the other side, and if you get in a fight with them and the enemy pours in a pretty heavy fire, they will go away with them." General Pike said that Drew's men were eager to fight the Yankees, but did not wish to fight against their brothers the Creeks.

The Watie and Drew units were kept separated to prevent bloodshed, because of their intense hatred of each other. Conflict between the two Cherokee Regiments prevented them from cooperating in the Cherokee Nation. In fact, Drew's Regiment had two enemies, the Union and Watie's Regiment.

By January 5, the Confederates stamped out all Federal resistance in the Creek Nation. Plainly, the 1st Cavalry, Brig. General Ben McCulloch's Division and the Indian Cavalry Brigade had succeeded in suppressing the Creek uprising, keeping the Indian Territory in the Confederacy. The victory proved that a force capable of rapid action was a definite asset to the army. It showed cavalry brigades were large enough and strong enough to track down and defeat the enemy.

The Cherokee nation was uneasy, the Indians now as divided as any border state. Large Union armies in Kansas and Missouri were on the move. Although the weakened Cherokee Nation was in easy reach, the Union had bigger game in mind. Brig. General Samuel Ryan Curtis had assumed command of the Federals on Christmas Day, 1861 and planned to drive the Confederates out of Missouri and Arkansas.

In an unusual winter campaign, Curtis chased Major General Sterling Price's Confederate Missouri State Guards from Springfield, Missouri before Confederate forces led by Brig. General Ben McCulloch, at winter camps in Missouri and Arkansas could come to his aid. Price and McCulloch had an extreme dislike for each other and this antagonism between the commanders enabled the Union forces to take control of southwest Missouri with little effort, because they met no cooperative resistance.

One of Pike's first acts of importance was to obtain funds for the Indians and on January 28, 1862, he wrote from Little Rock to Major Elias Rector, Superintendent of Indian Affairs at Fort Smith:

"I have $265,927.50 in specie. Of course I must stay with it...about 150 gamblers here, following up the Indian moneys. I enclose an order requiring passports, that will keep them out of the Nation...I have the $150,000 advance for the Cherokees, the $12,000 owed the Nation and the $10,300 due the Treaty Party of Stand Watie's...also the $50,000 advance for the Choctaws.

Pike had ordered uniforms for his Indians, but they never came. Their weapons were their own and, without regular provisions, lived on the country across which they marched and fought. Ross considered Watie's Cherokees as base, reckless and unprincipled, who domineered and trampled the rights of peaceable citizens. It was true that Indian Officers did not demand the strict discipline used by white officers, it was well known that Watie's troops were the best disciplined among the Indian commands. If his troops, later in the war, captured Yankee whiskey and drank too much, he would pour the remaining into the nearest stream.

In Mid February 1862, Curtis's Union Army chased Price's Missouri Militia into northwest Arkansas. Major General Earl Van Dorn, commander of the newly created Confederate Trans-Mississippi District, ordered Price and McCulloch to join forces with all Confederate units in the west to drive the

Union back. On February 25, Van Dorn ordered Brig. General Albert Pike to move his Indian Brigade to Bentonville, Arkansas to join them.

In late February 1862, Major General Curtis began moving his Federal troops south, following and harassing Gen. Sterling Price's Missouri Confederates, as they pulled back south out of Missouri. The stage was being set for the largest battle west of the Mississippi. All roads led now to Elkhorn Tavern (Pea Ridge to the Union). Price, extremely disappointed he had not received reinforcements from McCulloch and the 16th Arkansas Infantry, continued his retreat, with Curtis's Cavalry sniping at the rear, reaching Cross Hollow, Arkansas on February 25th. He kept moving south toward the Boston Mountains and destiny.

General Van Dorn's headquarters were then located in the Boston Mountains south of Fayetteville. Major General Earl Van Dorn sent orders out to Generals Price, McCulloch and Pike, Colonels Watie, Drew and McIntosh, to start moving their forces toward Fayetteville, timed to join Van Dorn's troops by March 7. Units involved were Col. Hebert's Louisiana Infantry, General McIntosh's Cavalry, General Pike's Indian Regiments, Watie's and Drew's Regiments, Col. Sims 9th Texas Calvary.

Pike was not pleased with these orders to move his Indian forces into Arkansas. The treaties he had worked so hard for with the Nations, specifically stated they would not be required to fight outside Indian Territory. Yet, the impending showdown between these two great armies in the West would surely affect the future of Indian Territory. Therefore, Pike prepared to follow his orders. The First Creek Cavalry Regiment and the First Seminole Cavalry Battalion refused to go until the Confederacy made its overdue treaty payments. Pike did not press the issue and left the

Territory with 800 men of the First and Second Cherokee Mounted Rifles.

With Watie and Drew's Regiments in Arkansas, the only military force left to defend the Cherokee Nation, were 22 Cherokees commanded by Captain Henry Chambers. This force, recruited March 3, 1862 guarded the now fat Cherokee treasury, as March 1, 1862, General Pike had paid the Cherokees $70,000 in gold and $150,000 in Confederate treasury notes, per the treaty.

Many of the Confederate Indians believed that Van Dorn's orders betrayed the treaties between their governments and the Confederate States. The treaties stated that no Indian troops were to be used outside the Indian Nations without the Nations' consent. So some of Indians felt they had not been asked to fight in Arkansas, but ordered to go.

Drew's Regiment received orders from Pike March 3, to move along Cane Hill Road to join Van Dorn's Army. Drew ordered a forced march with the Cherokee Mounted Rifles carrying only light equipment and the regimental baggage was to "travel at its own pace" so as not to hinder the troop's progress. He had about 500 men out of the 1000 plus on his muster roll in November 1861. The desertions from his regiment the previous December had severely reduced the effectiveness for the coming campaign.

General Pike and Watie's Regiment and Captain Olis G. Welch's Texans overtook Drew's column about six miles south of Bentonville. The First and Second Choctaw and Chickasaw still followed far behind, reluctant to fight in Arkansas. Pike, with Watie and Drew's Regiment pushed north. They still had not been paid for their services, and were not happy about fighting outside Indian Territory.

Elk Horn Tavern

Van Dorn's advance had pushed Union forces toward Elkhorn Tavern. This was a result of a 4-5 hour running battle with Pike's advance Guard. Union Commander, General Samuel Curtis had dug in overlooking Little Sugar Creek, expecting an attack by Van Dorn's army of 16,000 men and more than 60 cannon. Curtis had about 10,500 effective soldiers and 49 cannon. Although, he was outnumbered, Curtis's troops were more rested, because Van Dorn's had forced marched to Bentonville. The weather was also very cold, snow having fallen the day before, March 5. The sub-freezing temperature was hard on the Cherokee, as their supply wagons and equipment were still far behind.

Late afternoon, March 6, General Pike's Brigade reached Brig. General Ben McCulloch's Division. Pike camped within 2 miles of the main Confederate forces at Camp Stephens, at the junction of two roads, 7 miles northeast of Bentonville.

With attack plans set, Pike's Indian Brigade, with McCulloch's Texas and Arkansas divisions were to circle around to the north to cut the Union Army supply lines. About midnight Drew's Regiment and the rest of Pike's Brigade moved into position. A member of Price's Brigade later wrote of the Indians' movement,

"They came trotting into camp, yelling forth a war whoop that startled the Army out of its propriety. Their faces were painted for they were on the Warpath.Their long black hair qued in clubs hung down their backs, buckskin shirts, leggings and moccasins adorned with little bells and rattles, together with bright colored turkey feathers on their heads completed unique uniforms, not strictly cut according to military regulations. Armed only with Tomahawks and war clubs, and presented an appearance somewhat savage, but they were mostly Cherokees, cool and cautious in danger, active and sinewy in person, fine specimen of the Noble Red Man."

A Texan wrote, "On the way to the battlefield, we passed Pike's Indian Brigade, all of whom were painted in the horrid customs of their people." A Confederate surgeon wrote on the morning of the battle, he observed almost 300 Indians daubing their faces black with charcoal. A chief told him, when going into a fight, they painted their faces red, but when suffering from hunger, they colored black. It should be remembered that not all Cherokee were "civilized," or had adapted to the white man's way of dress. Many traditional Cherokees clung to the old customs and dressed accordingly. Although many had been educated in religious schools, the use of war paint and scalping were traditions hard to suppress.

General Curtis had thrown out scouts, spies, and Union citizens coming into his lines from the territory to keep him informed of the Southern movements. He had thrown forward detachments from various divisions, covering about twenty-five miles of his front, from Huntsville to Osage Mills. He withdrew them just in time to evade capture. Some troops had to retreat fighting to reach his position at Sugar Creek. He strengthened his position by dropping trees across the roads on his flank to slow Van Dorn's advance.

Trees cut down by the Union to block movement of horses, wagons, and artillery delayed the Confederates, messages not received which caused backtracking and because of the intense cold and exhaustion caused by long marches, troops were trying to cross Little Sugar Creek on a makeshift bridge to avoid fording the creek. The delays gave Union scouts a chance to report the Confederate flanking movement, so that the Confederates lost their element of surprise. Their troops did not get into position until 10:00 AM and fighting had already started around Elkhorn Tavern.

.Drew's Regiment and the Indian Brigade saw some Union troops about 300 yards away. These were the advance units of elements of Colonel Peter J. Osterhaus's 1st Division, consisting of Captain Gustavus M. Elbert's flying battery of 3 James Rifles in the Missouri Light Artillery, 2nd Company, 1st Missouri Regiment and the Fremont Husars (4th Missouri Cavalry), the Benton Husars (5th Missouri Cavalry Regiment). The Union force's orders were to meet the flanking Confederates and delay them until reinforcements arrived.

About noon, regular units of the Confederate Cherokee began their first action outside Indian Territory. While Brig. General James McQueen McIntosh's brigade charged the Federals in a large field to the east, Pike drew his 1,000-man brigade and Colonel Sim's 150-200 Texans into a line near some woods as the 3-gun Union battery opened on the Confederate Column.

The Union guns of Elbert's Missouri Light Artillery opened fire into the wooded area where Watie and Drew's troops were. The range of the gunners was good but not deadly. Watie's troops dismounted on the right flank of the Confederate line, on the left was Sim's Texans and in the middle were Welch's Texans, and Drew's still in the saddles, Pike ordered a charge by his full line. With war whoops and Rebel yells, the Cherokees and Texans erupted in the attack. The two Cherokee Regiments swept forward along with part of the Ninth Texas of Lt. Col Quayle, the bearded, wild-eyed Texans matched strides through the small brush with Watie's Warriors. Brandishing shotguns, rifles, tomahawks, knives and bows and arrows, the Indians charged with wild shrieks and war cries and hit Osterhaus's Calvary Regulars before he had a chance to pull his flying artillery back.

His gunners panicked and fled, and almost simultaneously, McIntosh had charged the Federal line from the North, breaking completely through it. Osterhaus's Calvary then broke and fled back through Leetown. The Indian Regiments swarmed over the guns routing the Union Calvary, firing as they ran. Only four horses of the battery remained on the field after the charge of Watie and Drew's men, the others running off with the caissons. Pike was not able to send the guns to the rear at this time due to lack of horses and harnesses.

The charge by the Indians and Texans killed about 30-40 Blue Coats. Highest loss of the Confederates was Drew's Regiment with two dead, 1 wounded. The Texans had one dead, one wounded. One Yankee artilleryman was laying stretched out between some of the artillery pieces, apparently dead. One of the full blood Cherokees "took out his knife, got his fingers into the Yankee's hair, cut out and jerked off a scalp about the size of a dollar. Thus resurrected, Mr. Yank got him on his legs in a hurry and ran like a quarter horse.....Not a gun was fired after him, but a yell went up....Go it Yank, we have a lock of your hair!"

With the cannons captured, there was confusion and chaos for a few minutes, which gave Osterhaus's First Division time to move two additional artillery units up and begin firing on the disorganized Cherokee and General McIntosh's brigade. The Confederates could not hear the orders yelled over the bedlam, to turn the cannon on the Union. Osterhaus had rallied his troops, along with the Benton and Fremont Hussars, 36th Illinois volunteers and Capt. Hoffman's 3-gun battery. The artillery opened fire checking the Confederates advance. After a few shells, the Cherokee pulled back to the trees. They had not been trained to fight in open fields in the formal military manner in the fashion of the day, but to fight individually, in the cover of woods, frontier fashion. Watie and Drew's Regiments took shelter in the trees with shells falling around them.

The battle was furious and began to tilt to the Union. McCulloch's 16th Arkansas and Hill's Regiment charged, but the volleys drove them back. About 1:30, several cavalry units advanced toward the Union, Drew's forces joined to advance with the Texans. They were to attack on foot to join in the fight "in their own fashion." Some of Watie's Cherokees wheeled two of the cannon into the trees. The furious onslaught continued, gun smoke swirled over the battlefield, mixed with war whoops, Rebel yells, the screams of the wounded from both sides. The cold was forgotten in the heat of battle.

About 3:00, Pike learned that General Ben McCulloch, veteran Indian fighter and Texas Ranger, had been killed while scouting the Union lines. General James McQueen McIntosh, McCulloch's second in command, had also been killed in the vicious fighting. General Pike found himself senior officer of the Confederate right wing. He did not know the roads in the area or the Confederate battle plan as he had not been in contact with McCulloch or McIntosh during the battle, and did not know where all the Confederate troops were located. He had no formal training as commander of a large body of troops, so did not know just how to handle the situation.

Pike rode up on a small hill, to try to see where his troops were. He saw part of the troops withdrawing toward the Bentonville-Little Sugar Creek Road, gathered what Confederate troops he could find, and moved to join Van Dorn and Price around Elkhorn Tavern. He ordered the captured cannons burned because he could not move them. The gunpowder exploded, killing several Cherokee. Watie's regiment was with Pike, but Drew's regiment did not receive the message, so when they found a large Union force advancing, beat a hasty retreat west to Camp Stephens about 2 hours away.

At Camp Stephens, Drew's Regiment found the Confederate supply train and 200 of Colonel Douglas H. Cooper's First Choctaw and Chickasaw Regiment and Colonel Daniel N. McIntosh's First Creek Regiment. They were supposed to have joined Pike's Brigade earlier, but because of dissension about fighting in Arkansas and no pay, they arrived too late for the first days fighting. Most of these Regiments were still in Indian Territory and had decided not to fight in Arkansas.

The first complete day of battle, the seventh, was probably a draw, all things considered, with perhaps even a slight edge to the Confederates. There was no Federal advance on the line and the Union supply and communications were in chaos. The Confederates had deployed along the ridge above the Union.

When darkness fell, the Federal right under Colonel Carr had been forced back several miles, with heavy casualties, and had to yield to the enemy Elkhorn Tavern and the heavily timbered one hundred acres southwest of the Tavern and west of the Fayetteville or Wire Road.

General Curtis had parked his supply train in a large field west and southwest of the timbered area, with the teams still hitched, ready to move at a moments notice. After darkness fell and the field was quiet, he was able to furnish his troops and animals with food. The troops rested during the night with guards set out to keep an eye on the movements of the Confederate troops.

Despite the deaths of Slack, McCulloch, and McIntosh, and the capture of Louisiana commander Louis Herbert, the Confederates slept that night content of victory. Drew's Indians left and was already on their way back to Indian Territory.

Drew's men stayed with the supply train along with the other Confederate troops and did not fight on the second day, March 8, 1861 at Elkhorn Tavern. The wagon train was waiting orders to move up. The commander of the wagons sent a scout to locate McCulloch, for orders. In the meantime, McCulloch, before he died had sent a rider with orders to move the wagons forward. The messengers missed each other, and as soon as the courier from Elkhorn Tavern arrived, the wagons started moving toward the battle. Drew's Regiment followed the wagons as escort. The morning of the eighth, Curtis's artillery opened effective fire against the Confederates on Pea Ridge; the roar of the cannon sounded for several miles from the scene. Firing from both sides was quite heavy for some time. Finally, get the range, Curtis's artillery, with deadly accuracy, succeeded in silencing the Rebel guns and the Southerners started pulling off the ridge and falling back. Federal rifles began to take a vicious toll against them, pitting superior firepower against poorly equipped Southern troops, many armed with only short-range shotguns and pistols. Curtis knew victory was leaning his way and threw everything he had available into the infantry charges, both at Pea Ridge and beyond Elkhorn Tavern. The infantry hit hard and continuously.

The Confederate Artillery was low on ammunition and could only fire occasionally while the Union fired volley after volley into the Confederate lines. The Confederates were losing badly as they only had the supplies they had carried in the first day. The supply train, ordered forward, moved toward Elm

Springs where they camped the night of March 8, north of Bentonville. The next morning it arrived at Elm Springs, and Drew's Regiment, the First Creek Regiment, and the First Choctaw and Chickasaw Regiment, headed back to Indian Territory. They felt they had fulfilled their mission for the Confederacy in Arkansas and that their presence was needed in the Indian Nations.

Not receiving the much needed supplies and reinforcements, the main Confederate force fled southward after being badly mauled during the two day battle of Pea Ridge. Watie's men held their position on the ridge as long as possible without being overwhelmed. The Confederate Army was routed and in full retreat in three directions. With Pike and his staff cut off from the main body of Indian troops, they wandered in the hills. Stand Watie, his command in good order, helped cover the Rebel withdrawal, as did Jo Shelby. Sigel, who was following the deceptive Shelby, became so confused about the Confederate strength he warned the victorious Curtis that Van Dorn might yet rally and surround the Federals.

General Curtis took about 10,500 troops total into the battle. He reported his lasses at 203 killed, 980 wounded, and 201 missing. Added also should be two officers and seven men killed, four officers and fifty-seven men wounded of Colonel John S. Phelps' Regiment of Missouri Volunteers. General Van Dorn reported his strength at 16,000 just before the battle began, and casualties of 800-1,000 killed and wounded and 200 prisoners.

Union sources reported Van Dorn's forces lost 1,100 killed, 2,500 wounded, and 1,600 captured or missing. A Confederate Surgeon listed the losses at 185 killed, 525 wounded, 300 captured. Among those captured at Elkhorn Tavern from Drew's Regiment were Captain Richard Fields, exchanged 5-17-1862;

James P. Evans, Surgeon, paroled 6-23-1862; Walter N. Evans, (Dr. Evan's son), Hospital Steward, paroled 7-11-1862 and Private James Priddy, who was taken to the Union POW camp at Alton, Illinois, where he died 3-30-1862. Karrne Brown, Company. M Second Choctaw and Charles Potts were captured and sent to Jefferson Barracks in St. Louis, where Brown died November 25 and Potts died December 16, 1863.

Had the Kansas forces of five or six thousand at Fort Scott for operations into Indian Territory been ordered to Pea Ridge, the Confederate forces might have been destroyed, ending further efforts of Southern Forces to control Missouri. However, politics kept them out.

On March 9, General Van Dorn asked General Curtis to bury the dead at Elkhorn Tavern and asked that a Confederate burial party be allowed on the field under a flag of truce. Curtis agreed and both sides attended the dead at Elkhorn tavern.

In burying the dead, they found that many had been scalped. General Curtis sent a message to General Van Dorn, regarding this, Van Dorn answered he would investigate the charges, and gave Curtis his apologies for the situation. He criticized Pike for losing control of his Indian troops after their capture of the Union artillery and looked down on them as savages who scalped and mutilated the dead. Later, when Drew's men deserted after the battle at Locust Grove, they told the Federals that the killing of the white rebels by the Indians in the Pea Ridge fight was determined before they went into battle. In the excitement of the initial Indian charge and capture of the Federal battery, the Drew Indians temporarily halted their plans to turn against the Confederates.

In his official reports of the battle, Van Dorn still refused acknowledge Pike and his command. He and some of his officers exaggerated the role that the

Cherokee withdrawal had on the outcome of the battle. Incidentally, Van Dorn had made a name for himself before the war as an Indian fighter, leading US cavalry against the Comanche in Texas. Needless to say, he was no admirer of the Indian Culture.

The highest credible number of scalpings of Union soldiers found is eight, although many report much more. These soldiers were from the Third Iowa Cavalry, privates; David Carroll Company B; Carroll Foster Company A (reported scalped but not found); Casper Freitch Company B (reported scalped but not found); Elisha Ham Company A; Spence Miner Company D and Sgt. Ralph Millard Company C.

Although the Cherokee played a significant part in taking the gun battery the first day, historians would later ignore their presence and credit only the Texans. Many of the Union dead were scalped and mutilated by the Cherokee in the heat of battle; a fact later given wide spread publication in Northern papers. The full bloods in Drew's Regiment blamed the mixed-bloods in Watie's, but the blame was equal. The scalpings can be laid directly at his feet, as he had ordered the Confederate Indians into Arkansas. Some historians also say the Texans were responsible for some of the scalpings.

There were also Cheyenne present at Elkhorn Tavern. George and Charley Bent, sons of the Santa Fe Trail trader William Bent and his Cheyenne wife, Owl Woman, (Tsistsistas) had been in Saint Louis in 1861 when Nathaniel Lyon, the commander of the USA Arsenal there, captured an encampment of Missouri militia. The Bents joined the Missouri State Guard and fought with Confederate troops.

A few days after Elkhorn Tavern, Pike found Drew and the other two Regiments waiting for him at Cincinnati, Arkansas. Until then, Pike had not known what had happened to the rest of his Indian Brigade.

Watie's Regiment returned to the Cherokee Nation after discovering the Confederate wagon train they were supposed to escort from Elm Springs had already left.

After the March 7, 1862 battle at Elkhorn Tavern in Arkansas, the Confederate authorities diverted all possible forces and equipment to the east side of the Mississippi. Thus, the Indian Nations were left with scarcely any protection from their Confederate allies. Pike was outraged and viewed this as another broken treaty with his troops. The Confederate government had pledged to protect the tribes that had signed their treaties of alliance. Van Dorn commandeered the arms and equipment ordered by Pike for his troops for his white troops. Pike became bitter and refused to follow future orders from any high ranking Confederate officers, except at the top levels from Richmond. He became a Rebel among Rebels, setting up his own little Confederacy in Indian Territory.

General Pike developed his own strategy for the defense of Indian Territory. He felt his force was too weak to defend the Northern region, yet he knew there would likely be a Union invasion soon. With the odds against him, he wanted to make sure the Union invasion would be long and costly. He set up headquarters in southern Choctaw Nation, near the Red River, and sent his Creek and Seminole troops to guard their own Nations. Watie and Drew were to act as advance guard, watching over the Cherokee Nation.

The worn and weary Cherokee returned to Indian Territory. Many were furloughed to go home, rest and get their crops planted, because without the crops, many of the Indian families and Confederate troops would go hungry the next winter.

The Indian Territory was wide open and they expected a Union invasion. The furloughed soldiers were to rejoin their units when the Union came. On

March 22, parts of Drew's troops were sent to Webber's Falls to guard supplies. Chief Ross was uneasy about his Regiment (Drew's) being away from the Capitol. With the Cherokee Treasury and records not guarded, he wanted some of Drew's troops ordered to his home at Park Hill. Most of Pike's Brigade was in the Choctaw Nation near Red River. For all practical purposes, Watie and Drew's partially furloughed Regiments were left to defend the Cherokee Nation.

By spring 1862, Kansas was desperate to get rid of the thousands of refugee Indians in camps there. These Indians were in very bad shape and wanted help to return home, even offering to serve in the army in order to get home. Therefore, the invasion of Indian Territory, with the primary objective to escort these refugees home, included the take over of Indian Territory for the Union.

Recruiting officers were sent among the refugees in Southern Kansas, began recruiting between LeRoy Kansas and the Osage Catholic Mission on the Neosho River, and nearly two full regiments were organized and prepared for the field as to arms and equipment. The government had on hand at Fort Leavenworth enough of the long barreled "Indian rifles" to arm part of the troops. They used a percussion cap instead of flint and powder pan and fired a round bullet that was quite effective at close range. The Indians generally preferred this to the army muskets that were in use.

The Federal expedition outfitted at Fort Scott, started to the Cherokee Nation on March 6, 1862. It was designated the "Indian Expedition" and was under the command of Colonel William Weer, who wrote from LeRoy, Kansas on the thirteenth of June , "John Ross is undoubtedly with us and will come out openly when we reach there."

This force included the Tenth Kansas Infantry, under Colonel Weer; Ninth Wisconsin Infantry,

Colonel Frederick Salamon; Second Ohio Cavalry, Colonel Charles Doubleday; Sixth Kansas Cavalry, Colonel William R. Judson; Ninth Kansas Cavalry, Colonel Edward Lynde; Captain Rabb's Second Indiana Battery; Captain Allen's First Kansas Battery; and two Indian regiments consisting of Cherokee, Creek and Seminole.

Doubleday would not wait for Weer and marched his troops out of Fort Scott on June 1. The Indian Expedition rapidly approached from the north by way of Humboldt, Kansas and Cowskin Prairie, Cherokee Nation. They crossed into Indian Territory with a force of about 2,500 men, anxious to singlehandedly whip all the Johnny Rebs in the Confederacy.

Chapter Five

By the middle of April, Major Pegg placed some troops at Park Hill to guard the chief and the government. Captain John Porum Davis' company was sent from Webber's Falls to guard supplies at Cantonmont. The men from Drew's Regiment were now widely dispersed in camps and homes throughout the Cherokee Nation. Watie's Regiment, stationed on the Northern border, orders were to make raids into Kansas and Missouri to harass troops there.

Neosho, Missouri

Before leaving Baxter Springs, Colonel Weer had information through his scouts that a Confederate force of Indians and whites were camped at Round Grove, on the east side of Grand River, about 20 miles away. His troops struck camp and crossed into Indian Territory, marched south on the Old Military Road to Fort Gibson. The command crossed the Neosho River at Hudson's Ford, turned east, and crossed the Grand River heading for Cowskin Prairie. It camped in a grove where there was good water. The army, now in enemy territory, posted sentries to prevent a surprise attack.

Colonel Jewell took a detachment east to the state line and south ten to fifteen miles. Officers talked to a number of Cherokee who informed them the Confederate forces under Rains, Coffee, Clarkson, Hunter had been in the area for several weeks with about fifteen hundred men, and Colonel Watie had three to four hundred Cherokee troops. They also told that this Southern force had recently made a raid into Missouri as far as Neosho.

Union Major J. M. Hubbard, commanding the First Battalion of First Missouri Cavalry headed a scouting party southwest out of Cassville, Missouri -

146 men and a six pounder brass howitzer - arrived at Elk Mills, Indian Territory on April 25, about a mile north of Watie's base camp at Cowskin Prairie. Unable to find the main body of Watie's force (Watie only had about 40 men with him) started his return to Missouri. The sharp-eyed Cherokee scouts watched Hubbard's movements. They followed as he returned toward Neosho, Missouri. By morning, Watie had collected about 140 of his men plus about 60 troops of the Independent Command of Col. J. T. Coffee's Missouri State Guard.

Watching them from a hill was a lone figure. Watie sat on his pony planning his attack. A seventeen-year-old mixed blood scout, Private John Martin had brought word the enemy was about 300 strong. Dismounting his men, he planned to attack at two points, one point with about 125 of his men and the second point covered by Colonel Coffee's troops.

The Confederates moved quietly into position and at his quiet command, attacked just after dawn. They rushed into the camp surprising and killing the pickets, other northern troops killed and wounded, included several officers. Most of the Union casualties were a result of the first assault.

Although surprised. Hubbard rallied his troops and the cavalry attacked with their new Colt six shooter rifles, forced the Rebels back into the wooded area where their attack started. The enemies repeating rifles were far superior to Watie's, troops' shotguns, handguns, and single shot rifles. Another problem, Coffee did not support Watie's attack, the Confederate Missourians fading back into the woods instead of pressing the second prong of attack.

Watie's Regiment, with Colonel John T. Coffee's Missourians skirmished the better part of the day near Neosho, Missouri against the 1st Missouri Cavalry with losses of 30 killed and wounded and 62 taken prisoner,.

Watie's troops withdrew back toward Cowskin Prairie and the Union continued their withdrawal to Cassville.

Supplies and ammunition was difficult for Watie, operating independently as he was. The Regiment was nearly out of the brass percussion caps used for firing the percussion lock long rifles and pistols, about sixteen kegs of black powder was left, and several pigs of lead.

Watie's reputation was growing now. As a scout and guerilla leader, it was enhanced in late May in another and larger combat near Neosho, Missouri. On May 31, Colonel Coffee's Missouri troops and Watie's Regiment badly mauled a Union scouting party of 500 from the 14th Missouri Cavalry and 10th Illinois Cavalry, under Union Colonel John M. Richardson. The war cries and Rebel Yells of the Confederate Indians made the Union horses virtually unmanageable and after three rounds of fire, the Federal forces broke and ran in confusion.

Captain Park's Confederates made their victory a more telling one by pushing on into the town of Neosho and capturing two Union flags, one that had only been raised on the Neosho courthouse steeple a short time before the battle. The Confederates killed or wounded ten Union soldiers, suffering the loss of one man in Coffee's unit, and captured five wagons and teams, arms, horses, tents and the entire enemy's baggage. Watie's First Regiment, Cherokee Cavalry, had made itself a force to be reckoned

Colonel Richardson had managed to escape on foot through the woods and hiding in a Union sympathizer's home on Diamond Grove Prairie. His scattered force retreated in disorganization back to Mount Vernon. Richardson was not soon to forget Watie's men, as his failure to resist the Confederate Cherokee's attack was to result in his investigation by the Union General commanding Southern Missouri.

Colonel Cooper, headquartered in Skullyville, ordered the two Cherokee Regiments to muster what men they could and take up a position on Telegraph road between Evansville and Maysville, Arkansas. They were to invade the Union held Southwest Missouri, using all but 2-4 companies of Drew's Regiment, which were to guard the funds, Archives and authorities of the Cherokee Nation at Park Hill.

Stand Watie's troops had now become the advance guard of the Indian Territory. With his typically rapid response to assigned responsibility, he immediately set up his scouting lines and patrols, keeping a flow of information south to Pike in the Choctaw Nation.

Cowskin Prairie

Establishing his base of operations at Cowskin Prairie, on the far northwestern portion of the Cherokee Nation, Watie rapidly came to grips with the Union forces. He monitored Union movements, whether it was Union General Curtis in the east to turn back a threatened attack by Van Dorn, or the Federal forces, Cavalry from Fort Scott, Kansas or Springfield, Missouri on the Missouri - Kansas borders. Watie did his best to meet on every occasion possible although he had only about 200 troops with him. He had furloughed the others after Pea Ridge, and many of the 200 were scouting along the northern border.

Doubleday's assembled force reached Shoal Creek on June 6. Scouts reported there was a Rebel camp on Cowskin Prairie, which was east of the Grand River along the Missouri-Arkansas border. The Colonel took about 1000 men, infantry, Cavalry, and artillery and marched down the Spring River toward Watie's camp at Cowskin Prairie. Before Cooper's orders to invade Missouri could be carried out by Watie and

Drew, Doubleday's force reached the Grand River the evening of June 6. Watie's camp with about 400 men was three miles away at Watie's saw mill. The rest of his Regiment was not expected back for a few days. Under cover of artillery, the Union force attacked exploding the quiet camp scene at sundown, with flashes of thunder and lightening. The Southern troops dropped their meager dinner rations and scrambled for cover. Watie's good friend and aide, Lt. Colonel William Penn Adair was captured. Watie's troops, who were camped with a force of Missouri Cavalry under Col. John T. Coffee, fled as bullets flew and in the distance the drum beat signaled more troops were coming. They scattered into the night leaving supplies and 500-600 head of cattle and horses, evading capture.

The Union troops' morale soared when they discovered the force they had just scattered without the loss of one man, was none other than Watie's Cherokee Mounted Rifles, the best Confederate Indian unit in the Territory. Nevertheless, that action also gave early warning of the Federal invasion.

With Colonel Stand Watie charging down the dirt roads, across the countryside with their mixed blood Rebel Yell in southwest Missouri and the Nations, Union commanders were growing tired of hearing tales of the iron hoofs and constant clang of Watie and his men.

Soon after the action at Cowskin Prairie, a courier arrived with orders for Doubleday to march to Baxter Springs, a Union post established across the Kansas line, and meet Weer's troops. Meanwhile, Weer was having the most frustrating and challenging time of his career, trying to recruit and train his two Indian regiments. The Indians were not used to the white man's way of training and military discipline. The command structure was confusing as to whose orders to obey, their chiefs' or their new unit officers.

Brigadier General Pike had made his headquarters at Camp McCullough near Red River since the battle of Pea Ridge and June 23, 1862 Colonel Douglas Cooper was given command of the Confederate units north of the Canadian River. Colonel J. J. Clarkson appointed as Confederate commander in the Cherokee Nation on June 26, ranked Colonels Watie and Drew, and independent of Brigadier General Pike.

On June 26, Lt. James Phillips, acting assistant Adjutant with Doubleday, wrote Chief Ross about the pending invasion.

"I have learned from your friends with me, that you and your people are truly loyal to the government of the United States, but from stress of circumstances have not been able to carry out your loyal principles during the present unholy rebellion. Speaking for Colonel Weer, he said my purpose is your protection and to relieve you and your country from your present embarrassment and to give you and all your friends an opportunity to show their loyalty to the United States Government."

With the coming of summer in the Cherokee Nation, the Confederate Indian Regiment was still serving without pay or promised arms, ammunition, clothing and supplies. In the eyes of many Cherokee, the Confederacy had broken their treaty. Some of the Cherokee had never officially been mustered in to the army. They were still undisciplined, armed mostly with only squirrel rifles, shotguns, and mounted on ponies. Many could not speak or write English and understood little about the Confederacy. They were still afraid of being sent east of the Mississippi to fight as many of the Texas Units had been. The prairies covered with the cattle of the Cherokees had no other food available locally. However, from this date, cattle rustling became so popular with the Kansans that before the end of the war cattle became a rare sight in the Nation.

As the Union forces gathered to invade the Cherokee Nation, parties of pro-Union Indians arrived daily in Kansas to join the newly mustered Indian Home Guards Regiments. The First Kansas Indian Home Guards was composed of eight companies of Creeks, 2 companies of Seminole. The Second and Third Regiments were predominately Cherokee along with Creeks, Choctaws, Chickasaws, and Osages. The Regiments were staffed with white officers, the Second Regiment had 66 officers, and 1800 privates, the 3rd had 52 officers and 1437 privates, totaling 3388 men. . On June 28, the Indian Expedition began its move into the Cherokee Nation. The First Regiment commanded by Col. Robert W. Furnas, designated as the First Indian Home Guard, contained the Creek and Seminole who had fought under O-pothle-yohola. The Second Indian Home Guard commanded by Col. John Ritchie had Cherokees, Delaware, Osages, Quapaw, Caddos, Shawnees, Kansa Indians, and Kickapoo.

Colonel Weer now had some 6,000 men in his Indian Expedition. The Second Kansas Indian Home Guards had many Cherokee, including the deserters from Drew's Regiment. With the invading Union Indians, the Confederate Indians and families fled south into the Choctaw Nation

The Confederate Cherokee sent urgent demands for help. Chief John Ross was not successful trying to persuade General Pike to leave Fort McCulloch and go to meet the Union force. Stand Watie and John Drew appealed to the Confederate commander, Major General Thomas Hindman, in Arkansas for reinforcements. Hindman was trying to rebuild

Confederate strength in Arkansas through forced conscription and could spare no men. He had ordered Pike to send all his white troops to Arkansas and to take his Indian Brigade to reinforce Drew and Watie. At first Pike refused, but later sent Colonel Cooper and several companies of the Choctaw and Chickasaw Regiment to Watie, and some Arkansas Infantry and artillery to Little Rock. Both detachments were slow in reaching their destinations and Hindman decided the stubborn Pike would not comply, so relented, and sent a battalion of Missouri Cavalry under Colonel J. J. Clarkson to defend the Cherokee Nation, and if possible, raid into Kansas.

Colonel Weer boldly decided to attack Watie and Drew's camps and split his forces accordingly. The stage was now set for a bold Union strike into the heart of the Cherokee Nation. There were skirmishes with Weer's force as they pushed into the Cherokee Nation. Many of the Loyal Indians that had fled to Kansas followed the Indian Expedition back into Indian Territory, believing they would be able to go home protected by the United States.

Spavinaw Creek/Locust Grove

On July 3rd, Col. Watie's men, about 300-400 including Major Broke Arm and his Confederate Osage, were camped near Spavinaw Creek when scouts brought word that the Federals were heading their way. Knowing he could not take on Colonel L. R. Jewell and the Sixth Kansas Cavalry, his troops fell back. It resulted in a running fight as hundreds of horses galloped across the hot dry prairie, gun smoke mixing with the dust. Watie's troops then split off in different directions making it difficult for the Sixth Kansas to overtake the whole force. That same day the Ninth Kansas Cavalry and the First Indian Home Guards reached Col Clarkson's unfortified Confederate camp just before sunrise, near Locust Grove.

Weer had adjusted his march to arrive just at daybreak, capturing several of the Confederate pickets some distance out from the camp. He had the Southern force surrounded before they knew he was there. Firing awakened them, though they tried to escape, Federal forces tightened the cordon making escape impossible.

Watie did not have a chance to warn Clarkson. They silently surrounded the camp and took aim at the tents and blankets on the ground. The surprise attack came a little before dawn. The early morning erupted with panic, the troops caught in a deadly hail of gunfire, as the wraith of the Federal government fell upon them. The battle raged through the surrounding woods and brush as Union forces pursued the scattering Confederates all day. Col. Clarkson surrendered 100 of his troops, mostly Missourians. All his baggage, 60 wagons of powder and supplies, recently arrived from Fort Smith, lost. Those that had escaped fled to Tahlequah, spreading more panic.

Locust Grove was near Grand Saline, the salt works. The next day the prisoners and captured wagon train moved to the west side of the Grand River, where they camped near the mouth of Cabin Creek. The Indians that took part in the expedition helped themselves to the captured loot, except for the army supplies. The supplies went the various departments for use, and the powder given to the Indian officers for the Indian's rifles.

Nearly all of Drew's regiment had been camped on Flat Rock Creek on the west side of Grand River, some twenty miles southwest of Locust Grove. Once again, most of Col. Drew's Pin Indians defected to the Union when they learned of Clarkson's defeat at Locust Grove. These new recruits, many of them veterans of Elk Horn Tavern, gave Weer enough additional troops to form the Third Indian home. William A. Phillips became Colonel of the Third Indian Home Guards, U. S. A.

To celebrate Independence Day and their victories at Cowskin Prairie, Saginaw Creek, and Locust Grove, the Union invasion forces camped at Cabin Creek and divided their Confederate bootie. Much of the captured clothing went to the refugee Indians traveling with them. The Union Indians sent messages to their friends who were still in the Confederate Army, requesting they join the Union forces. Because of Union victories in the nation, new recruits flocked into the Union camp on Cabin Creek. Many of these deserters were from Drew's Regiment. The new recruits were amazed at the military might of the Union Army. The jubilant Fourth of July celebration had many toasts to their bravery and boasted of their plans for total victory. Weer's little army seemed invincible that sunny, warm day.

By the morning of July 6, more than 600 Cherokees from Drew's Regiment, 1st Cherokee Mounted Rifles, had joined the Union forces. At this point for all practical purposes, the Confederate unit known as Drew's Regiment disbanded. A group of about 200 Cherokees led by Chaplain Lewis Downing also joined the Union. Reverend Downing was a staunch abolitionist. On July 8, about 300 Cherokees and 30 Negroes passed Ross's residence at Park Hill, waving a white flag on their way to join Weer.

On July 10, Colonel Weer marched his army farther south and set up camp on Flat Rock Creek near Grand River, 18 miles north of the Confederate-held Fort Gibson. He then sent a detachment of cavalry to take Tahlequah. After leaving Cabin Creek, the weather had become oppressively warm for the Northern troops and animals; no rain had fallen since the expedition had entered the Territory to revive the dying grass. The expedition seemingly not able to move forward of retreat, the troops day after day were sweltering in the almost tropical heat and no dispatches had been received from the supply train.

Captain Harris S. Greeno took one company of the Sixth Kansas Cavalry, and about 50 Indian soldiers, which was a part of the Indian expedition, arrived on July 15 at Tahlequah, and surrounded the town. He discovered there was not a single man left in the village so they entered Tahlequah and captured the Cherokee Capitol without firing a shot. They headed southeast and found Ross at his large plantation, Park Hill. Captain Greeno reported, "Chief Ross feels very badly on account of our not having any forces on this side of the river (Grand) for protection." Over two hundred members of Drew's Regiments were at Chief Ross' at the time and Captain Greeno went through the formality of arresting Chief Ross, Lieutenant Colonel William P. Ross, Major Thomas Pegg, First Lieutenants Anderson Benge and Joseph Chooie, Second Lieutenants Lacey Hawkins, Archibald Scraper, George W. Ross, Third Lieutenants Allen Ross, Joseph Cornsilk and John Shell. These troops immediately volunteered for service with Weer's Union forces.

Colonel Watie and the remainder of Clarkson's troops now south of the Arkansas River left the north nearly free of the Rebel command. Chief Ross, a prisoner of war on parole, was convinced he was finally rid of that despised half-breed, Stand Watie. He decided it was not safe to remain within riding distance - or shooting distance of the mixed bloods.

After duration of about 10 months all told, the Cherokee alliance with the South was, as far as the Principal Chief and the full bloods were concerned, at an end, and so was the treaty. The Ridge faction, led by Stand Watie and his nephew Elias Boudinot, continued loyal to its promises. Divided interests and divided councils worked havoc. The Cherokee country became the legitimate prey of both armies, Cherokee cattle the victims of constant rustling. The freed blacks had a share too, in the general robbery. Reports reaching the Federals stated they pillaged indiscriminately, from the Union Indians as well as the Rebels. The Federals regarded the Choctaw and Chickasaw lands as legal contraband. The private citizen acted as if he had as good a right to it as the government.

While Greeno was taking Tahlequah and Chief Ross, another contingent of Union forces, about 800 men, headed for Fort Gibson and the Arkansas. This was a typical July in Indian Territory, hot and dry. The creeks had shrunk to puddles of stagnant water. The Union had to rely on these dirty little pools, some with the cattle standing in them to ward off the heat and flies. The water had to be skimmed and boiled; even then, it was barely drinkable.

Union forces under Weer were camped 12 miles above Fort Gibson on the Grand River, an area in drought. The Confederates set fire to the prairie grass, forcing the Union troops to fight to save their camp in the hot July sun. By July 12, some 1500 new Cherokee recruits joined the Union force.

When Weer's force reached the Arkansas, south of the fort, they found Colonel Cooper's Choctaws and Chickasaws were already camped on the other side. After a few shots fired, the Union forces withdrew, heading back to their base camp at Flat Rock. When reaching camp, Col. Weer, spent the better part of the next ten days with a good supply of whiskey, not concerned with the rapidly deteriorating conditions of his camp. Supply trains from Fort Scott were long overdue, Confederate guerilla activities to the north of Flat rock were alarming. Stand Watie's forces had regrouped and again a constant threat to the Union supply line.

Discipline in the camp fell apart, hungry Indians left camp to go hunting and many did not return. White troops, on half rations, grumbled about their drunken commander and threatened mutiny. What had started as a great campaign rapidly fell into a disastrous expedition on a dead end road to defeat.

Colonel Frederick Salomon of the Ninth Wisconsin Volunteers arrested the drunken Colonel Weer at the camp on Cabin Creek on the charge of having conducted the command to a distant station where they were not in communication with the commissary department and practically out of provisions. Saloman, a former Prussian Army officer who had commanded German-American troops at Carthage and Wilson's Creek, Missouri took command of a mutinous Union army in Indian Territory, cut off from its supply lines and slowly being surrounded by the enemy.

Col. Saloman sent word of what he had done to General Blunt at Fort Leavenworth, and then prepared to march his miserable troops back to Kansas. He sent a detachment to Park Hill to take Ross into custody. He ordered the three Indian Regiments and one section of Kansas artillery to stay behind to fight Watie, Cooper and the various guerilla bands.

Having heard of the previous actions by the Federal forces, several hundred Cherokee, many being leading men in the Nation, gathered at Tahlequah and Park Hill to discuss the situation. They debated the matter, not seeming to get anywhere, so Captain Greeno decided to address them, giving his views of the situation. At a meeting of the leaders, he spoke.

"Leaders and people of the Cherokee Nation, I am here under orders of the Commanding Officer of the United States forces camped at Cabin Creek. It is an expedition of several thousand men, well supplied with cavalry, artillery and infantry, and sent by the Government into the Indian country to restore peace and tranquility among the Cherokee people, and to protect those who have lived up to the treaty relations with the Government. You have heard of the swiftness of our movements and of the first blow we have struck the enemy in the capture of Colonel Clarkson's command at Locust Grove a few days ago. We mean to keep up these blows until not an enemy organization shall find footing in your country. Last year the Federal Government did not have its forces organized until after the enemy, both Indian and white soldiers, had overrun your country, taken your property, and by threats and intimidation forced many of your people to take sides with south against their will and judgment. But I am able to tell you now that the Federal Government is rapidly getting its forces organized and equipped for an aggressive campaign on all front, and I may call your attention to the fact, if you have not already heard, where our arms have been completely successful recently in defeating large Southern armies and driving them from their strong positions with the loss of thousands prisoners and cannon and millions of dollars' worth of equipment."

"Commencing his mid-winter campaign, General Grant, after many bloody conflicts, drove the Confederate army out of Kentucky into their strongly fortified positions at Fort Donelson on the Cumberland River and Fort Henry on the Tennessee River, and after a short siege, compelled both places to surrender with more than 21,000 prisoners, including several generals, and with the loss of all their arms, supplies and equipment. This overwhelming success of the Federal arms caused the Confederate generals to retire their remaining armies to Corinth, Mississippi. "

"General Grant advanced in pursuit and took his army up the Tennessee River on transports, convoyed by gun boats armed with guns of heavy calibers to Pittsburgh Landing, where he disembarked his forces, 33,000 strong, and was soon attacked by the Confederate forces from Corinth under General Albert Sidney Johnston, 38,000 strong. After a desperate battle of nearly two days, defeated the Southern forces and drove them back to Corinth with a loss of nearly fifteen thousand men killed and wounded on both sides, General Johnston being among the slain. General Grant's forces moved forward from the victorious field and laid siege to Corinth, which had been strongly fortified and re-enforced by all the available Confederate forces in the West, and after more than a month's siege, the Confederate commander slipped out and retired further south, so that the Confederates were holding no position on that front, but were holding strong positions on the Mississippi River, the most northern of which was Island Number Ten. While General Grant's operations were going forth at Forts Donelson and Henry, and at Pittsburgh Landing and Corinth, the Confederate forces holding Island Number Ten were being fiercely attacked and besieged by Federal land and naval forces, and on the 7th of April, the last day of the battle of Pittsburgh Landing, compelled to abandon the Island, and endeavoring to escape, 5000 men and three generals were cut off and captured, and all their arms supplies and equipment, including more than 100 cannon fell into the hands of the victors. Continuing the Mississippi Campaign, the Federal Gunboat flotilla attacked d and defeated the Confederate Ram Fleet at Fort Pillow, and it retired to Memphis, where in the early part of June, it was again attacked by Admiral Walke, commanding the Federal Gunboat Flotilla and every vessel destroyed, except one, that escaped by flight down the Mississippi River. And now coming nearer your own homes, within cannon sound of the Cherokee Nation, the great three day battle of Pea Ridge was fought between the Federal forces of General Curtis, 10,000 strong, and the combined Confederate forces of Generals Van Dorn, Price and Pike, 16,000 strong, and you know the result. You know of the overwhelming defeat of the Southern forces who were driven from the field with the loss of three generals killed, McCulloch, McIntosh, and Slack, and of thousands of men killed, wounded and missing, and so demoralized that they were practically a disintegrated mass until they arrived at Van Buren for reorganization."

"While these operations were going on, Admiral Faragut, commanding the United States naval forces of the Gulf Squadron, passed the Confederate forts on the Lower Mississippi River, advanced up to New Orleans, and having the city under his guns, received its surrender leaving only two places of importance on the Mississippi River to the Confederates, Vicksburg and Port Hudson."

"These successes of the Federal arms are referred to show you that part of the Federal forces employed in those operations will be released for operations in Arkansas and the Indian country, and that it is the firm intention of the government to exercise its lawful authority in all this region, and to meet, engage and destroy all opposition as rapidly as practicable, and it has been pointed out to you the earnestness with which the Government has taken hold of the matter".

After concluding, the captain told the group, which had grown as he was speaking, that the government would not seek revenge on those, who under pressure had assumed a hostile attitude against the Government. They would be protected and forgiven. As the Captain returned to his camp, several hundred Cherokee, mostly from Drew's Regiment followed, and most joined the newly being organized Third Indian Regiment.

Chief Ross, with his friends and relatives, together with the national records and the two hundred fifty thousand dollars that had been received from the Confederate government, started north under a federal escort in the afternoon of the same day. They arrived at Fort Scott on August 7, 1862. Not withstanding the dire distress of most of the Cherokee refugees in southeastern Kansas, Chief Ross, his family and a few relatives, left one week later for Pennsylvania, where they established a "government in exile" and stayed during the remainder of the war. Ross was destined never to return to the Cherokee Nation. He traveled to Washington D.C. to explain his situation to President Lincoln, but received little sympathy. Ross died in Washington in 1866, maintaining that the Union forces, by abandoning Indian Territory in 1861, had forced him into the treaty with the Confederate States.

The actual government of the Cherokee was never in Philadelphia. It was held by a band of gallant fighters who rode under the Stars and Bars of the Confederacy. As soon as Ross had left the Territory, the Southern Cherokee had elected a new chief. There could only be one person for that role, intrepid, valorous and gallant, to rule the Cherokee Nation, Colonel Stand Watie! A letter dated September 15, appearing in the Confederate Record stated in part:

"In the meantime the serious feud existing between the Cherokee had terminated in the expulsion of Ross and the unsound faction and in the election of our tried friend, Stand Watie as their Chief."

General Blunt was quite angry that they had pulled out of Indian Territory. There was some talk of a court-martial for both Saloman and Weer, Blunt decided that an investigation would take more time than they could afford. However, the whole affair had the appearance of jealous insubordination, as both Colonel Weer and Colonel Saloman was shortly afterwards advanced in rank as if nothing had happened.

James Blunt was a tough Kansas abolitionist, who supported U.S. Senator James Lane. Lane was an outspoken anti-slavery Kansas Jayhawker, who had personally led bloody raids into Missouri to avenge similar raids into Kansas. Because of Blunt's association with Lane, he received his officer's commission.

The Federals had been in the Nation about a month and hundreds of refugee Indians had returned, thinking they would be protected by the Union forces, however, with the bulk of the white troops now camped in Kansas, or on their way there, the recently returned loyal Indians were now vulnerable to Confederate raids. The Union Indians were again on the defensive and afraid Colonel Douglas Cooper's army of Texans, Cherokees, Choctaws, Chickasaw, Creeks and Seminoles would sweep down on the outnumbered Union Indian Regiment and drive them out. Some of the Union Indian Home Guards began to desert and went home.

Some 180 Osage in a company of the Second Kansas Indian Home Guard, deserted to go buffalo hunting. Part of the First Kansas Indian Home Guard sent after the deserting Osages ran into a group of 125 Confederates on the Verdigris. The Rebels captured 14 Union soldiers and 1 Osage deserter. In disgust over the way the white Union troops had fled the Cherokee Nation, more of the Indian troops went home without leave.

As concerns in Kansas and Missouri grew, General Blunt pulled the Indian Expedition out of the

Cherokee Nation. This action ended the first Union invasion of the Indian nations. Guerilla warfare raged throughout the Cherokee Nation, as it became a hot bed of outlaws, renegades, and vigilantes from both sides. Intertribal warfare in the Cherokee Nation was fierce. Homes were burned, crops destroyed, livestock killed and unarmed men were gunned down because of their beliefs. It did not take long for the three Union Indian Regiments and the unlucky Kansas artillery to withdraw back to Kansas. Most of the Union families that had followed the troops also fled back to Kansas and the refugee camps they had left.

Units from Watie's command re-crossed the Arkansas when word came of the withdrawal of the white troops. They raided the Union Cherokee and on July 27, clashed with Phillips troops at Bayou Bernard near Park Hill. The Rebels turned back with Colonel Taylor and Captain Hicks of Watie's Command and two Choctaw captains killed.

There was such confusion in the Cherokee Nation in July 1862 that few knew what was actually happening or where the Yankee or Rebel Forces were. The pro-Union Cherokee extracted their revenge on the Confederate Cherokee, burning many homes and killing several. Confederate women and children forced to flee to safety camped with the Confederates in the Choctaw Nation. Food was scarce and with winter coming, not enough had grown for the troops and the refugees. Housing was another problem for the Confederate Indians. Although, the Choctaw sheltered what they could in their homes, many were facing the winter without protection.

Some members of Drew's Regiment that had remained loyal to the Confederacy, including Colonel John Drew, enlisted in other companies formed, becoming Company I of the Second Cherokee

Regiment. These included Captain John Porum Davis and Lt. Charles Drew.

By August, the bulk of the Union Indian Expedition was just south across the Kansas line. The Union Indian Regiments had suffered great losses from recent desertions and they retreated without provisions toward Fort Scott Kansas

Colonel Cooper commanding the Southern forces at Fort Davis received orders from General Hindman to move his forces consisting of the Choctaw and Chickasaw Regiments, the Creek Regiment, Colonel Watie's regiment of Cherokees, and a contingent of Texas troops to cross to the north side of the Arkansas River. They were to move north and east until they reached the Missouri forces under Shelby, Rains Cockrell.

Once again, General Pike received orders from Fort Smith, to march his Indian forces to join the Confederate army gathering at Fort Smith, to try an invasion of Union held Missouri. This was the last straw. Pike was outraged, resigned his commission and told his troops farewell, which including some hot remarks about the Confederacy.

"I have resigned the command of the Indian Territory and am relieved of that command. I have done this because I received an order to go out of your country to Fort Smith and Northwestern Arkansas, remain there and organize troops and defend the country; a duty which would have kept me out of the country (Indian Territory) for months...

Remain true I earnestly advise you, to the Confederate States and yourselves. Do not listen to any men who tell you that the Southern States will abandon you. They will not do it."

Complying with General Hyndman's orders, Pike turned over the troops and supplies to Cooper. When his resignation reached President Davis, he refused to accept it, so Pike returned to service until November, when he resigned again. Pike was accused of treason to the Confederacy and connected with a secret society of Unionists of Grayson and Cook Counties, Texas, where forty six were found guilty and hanged after a 'sort of' trial.

Col. Douglas Cooper called him either "insane or a traitor". Major General Thomas Hindman, who had ordered Pike's troops to Arkansas, heard of his remarks, and things almost worked for a court-martial of Pike. Arrested and taken to Fort Smith for the trial word came that his resignation had been approved. Therefore, Albert Pike simply walked away from the war and into the shadows of history and time.

Assuming command of all the Confederate Indian troops, Colonel Cooper immediately complied with Hindman's request crossing the border with his Choctaw and Chickasaws and about 200 Texas Cavalrymen. Working with Cooper, was Colonel Stand Watie, who was not particular where he killed Yankees and Pins. Altogether, there were about 2,000 troopers. Cooper rode into Missouri ahead of Hindman's main army in Arkansas and near Newtonia joined forces with about 2,300 other hard-riding troopers under the command of Col. Joseph "Jo" Shelby. Six artillery pieces added additional strength to the Rebel forces camped around the village.

After some discussions, the three Union Indian Regiments combined as the First Indian Brigade with Colonel R. W. Furnas as its commander. General Saloman was told the Indian Brigade could hold the Territory north of the Arkansas if he would leave a battery of artillery and honor their requisitions of supplies and ammunition.

Colonel Furnas dispatched his command for the protection of the loyal families in the area. He sent about two or three hundred to Fort Gibson to occupy the fort, but a day or two later evacuated as Colonel Cooper's force at Fort Davis a few miles away threatened to cut it off. He sent out a detachment under Colonel W. A. Phillips with the Third Indian Regiment to scout between Fort Gibson, Tahlequah and Park Hill where they skirmished with an equal force of Cooper's Indians under Lt. Colonel Thomas F. Taylor of Watie's Cherokee, during which Taylor, Captain Hicks and two Choctaw Captains, were killed and about fifty killed or wounded.

Cooper ordered the Confederate troops back south of the Arkansas and in the meantime, Furnas took the remainder of his command to Baxter Springs on the northern border of the territory, and Phillips joined him there. This left a large portion of the Territory open for the Indian forces to take over. Many of the Loyal families followed the troops north, knowing their leaving would leave them open to the revenge of the Southern forces, if they stayed home.

Occasional skirmishing with the Union troops had been going on before Cooper arrived. The Federal commander of the district, General John M. Schofield had heard of the buildup of Confederate forces near Newtonia and was gathering as many Federal troops as he could. Once again, the Rebel troops were threatening the state. Some of the skirmishes had been with Blunt's Second Indian Home Guards under Colonel Ritchie, who had come into the area by September.

Southwest Missouri was becoming an armed camp of warring forces. As soon as the Confederate forces were concentrated in considerable strength, Generals Blount and Schofield planned to move against them to see if they were strong enough to hold their ground. They did not believe their greatly exaggerated strength stated by the prisoners.

Carthage, Missouri

Early morning, September 11, 1862, a strong detachment of Colonel Shelby's Fifth Missouri Cavalry Regiment, under Captain Ben Elliot surrounded the camp of about 250 Indians and runaway slaves near Carthage, Jasper County, Missouri. The people in Carthage had sent word to Shelby, asking for help, as the Indians were terrorizing the town, robbing and burning homes at will. The Second Home Guards known for a severe lack of discipline, tended to pillage and plunder wherever they went. In this regiment were the Osage Warriors, who still plucked their hair leaving a scalp lock down the center. They were ferocious in both their appearance and dealings with any opposition. Their custom was to cut the heads off their victims, as well as take scalps. They still clung to their tribal ways and just did not conform well to a white man's way of military life. The Second Indian Home Guard had already developed the reputation of a severe lack of discipline and tended to pillage and plunder wherever they went.

When Captain Elliot's Cavalry charged into the camp from all sides, the Indians and allies scrambled for cover, offering little resistance. For two hours, the Missouri troopers hunted them through the woods around Carthage, killing many and capturing about 200 new rifles they had just received. The vengeance of the Confederates was not without cause. They found on the dead, the scalps of more than a dozen white victims, at least one being a woman.

On September 20, the 31st Texas Cavalry, under Colonel T. C. Hawpe and a unit of local guerillas under Major Tom Livingston attacked the main camp of the

Second Indian Home Guard, northwest of Carthage, at Shirley's Ford on the Spring River. Ritchie's Indians had along with them, wives and children, and as the attack began, they stampeded. At first, they were driven back, but made their stand stubbornly firing back at the Texans. The cavalry charges did not work, and Livingston and Hawpe argued as to how to handle the battle that resulted in Hawpe pulling out, leaving Livingston and his men to desperately fight their way out and keep their scalps.

Ritchie recorded he lost 12 to 20 men with 9 wounded and 22 Confederates killed. His Home Guards executed five civilians that day, 2 who turned out to be loyal Union men. Because of this incident along with the homes plundered by Ritchie's men Weer relieved him of command and arrested him. The reorganization of his regiment resulted in some warriors, including all the Osage, permanently discharged from Federal service.

Newtonia, Missouri

Colonel Cooper as Senior Confederate officer took command of all the Southern troops at Newtonia. On September 29, about 6,000 Federal troops reached the area sending 150 cavalry and 2 howitzers from the Union camp to probe the Confederates defenses. A brief skirmish followed then the Federals withdrew. The next morning the Union detachment, which included German immigrants, Wisconsin volunteers Kansas troops, the 3 Indian Home Guard Regiments, several companies of Wisconsin infantry, Kansas cavalry, and 3 cannon, attacked the Confederate force, unaware there were seriously large numbers of Rebel troops camped near. They openly marched over a ridge into the town, and fell into a Confederate trap.

The outnumbered Yankees had much more than they had bargained for. When Cooper's Choctaw and Chickasaw warriors under Lt. Col. Tandy Walker galloped through town in a howling charge, the Yankees broke. Walker's troops pursued them for about six miles, where they met General Saloman coming with his main force. Saloman rallied the troops, renewing the fight, but large numbers gave way in the evening forcing him to retreat. Federals had 50 killed, 80 wounded and 115 missing, Confederates had 12 killed 63 wounded and only three missing.

However, on October 3, General Scholfield entered the town with 18,000 troops, after a heavy artillery barrage. The stone fences that had helped earlier offered little protection for the Confederates. Cooper felt his defenses were vulnerable, signaled Lt. Colonel, R. C. Parks, who was commanding the Cherokee Rifles in Watie's absence, to provide a scattering fire. He signaled a retreat and the white Confederates retreated from Newtonia, to Arkansas, while Cooper's troops returned to Indian Territory. The Union army crossed the border into Arkansas and camped at the Pea Ridge battlefield. General Scholfield ordered General Blunt to march to Fort Wayne, where rumors were, Cooper's force was camped. They were afraid that Cooper and Watie would disrupt the flow of supplies and communications between the Union Army in northeast Arkansas and headquarters at Fort Scott. Blunt's mission, 'soundly defeat the Confederate Indians along the Arkansas-Indian Territory border.'

Blunt left his First Brigade, under General Salaman, at Pea Ridge, to scout the area while he took the Second and Third Brigades and headed for the Indian Territory and Arkansas border. His force reached Bentonville AR in the afternoon of October 21. He stopped just long enough for the troops to eat and feed the horses before moving out again. By 6:00, they were on the move again. The cavalry soon outdistanced the exhausted troops and stopped for some much-needed rest waiting for the others to catch up. When the lead units of the infantry caught up, they too fell by the side waiting for the rest to get there. They had been on a forced march for 36 hours; soon most of the Union Army was asleep along the Maysville Road.

General Blunt, ahead of his army with his staff, gave the order to move out. They passed by word of mouth; because he was afraid, the bugle would alert the enemy was near. The Second Kansas Cavalry, being the closet and having had more rest than the others, mounted and moved out behind the General.

They soon came upon a large nice home. Blunt quickly disguised himself as a Confederate soldier, escaping from the Union army, looking for the Confederate lines. His act soon convinced the lady of the house, whose husband was serving with Cooper, that his act was true. She informed him that the main Confederate camp was 3 miles past Maysville at Fort Wayne. Blunt returned to his staff down the road and went on toward Maysville with what he thought was his entire force.

Fort Wayne

At dawn on the 22nd, Blunt rode back to see if his force had caught up and was shocked to find only the one unit of Kansas Cavalry. He sent a messenger back down the road with orders for all troops to move up "double quick." Nevertheless, Blunt proceeded with his surprise attack with only three companies of cavalry, hoping to hold the enemy until his force could catch up.

Blunt attacked Cooper's troops on Beatty's Prairie nearby. The surprised Confederates went on the defensive, not realizing how small Blunt's force was. Soon additional Union cavalry rode onto the field including the rest of the Second Kansas with their two mountain howitzers. A thunderous artillery duel began between the two sides. Cooper then sensed how small Blunt's force was and started to flank the Union army. At that point, Colonel Phillips, the Third Indian home Guard, and the Sixth Kansas arrived and blocked their attempt. Blunt ordered an advance and soon the Rebels' horses came into the sights of Yankee Cavalry Rifles. The Confederates were defeated, their artillery captured and the Third Indian Home Guard and the Sixth Kansas pursued Cooper and Watie's Rebels through the fall countryside. Confederate losses were 6 killed, 30 wounded, and 26 missing. Blunt's forces had five killed and 5 wounded. Blunt's forces returned to Maysville, just across the Arkansas line showing off their trophy, a captured Rebel Battle flag.

Tonkawa Creek/Wichita Agency/Fort Cobb

Most Delaware under Black Beaver, located at the Wichita Agency in the western part of Indian Territory, collaborated with the Union. Black Beaver was a valuable Union scout, according to dispatches from both Union and Confederate.

During September 1862, there were rumors around Fort Cobb agency that Shawnees, Osages, Delaware and others who sympathized with the Union or hated Leeper were coming south to wipe out the Tonkawa and kill all the Confederate officials at the agency. Mr. Leeper, who had just returned from a business trip to Texas, promptly departed again with his family. He intended to return when he had them to a safe place. Horace Jones was in charge and he paid little attention to the reports, believing his Indian friends would warn him before an attack. He did not even become alarmed when he found out the Caddos were having secret meetings.

Meanwhile the Caddos kept telling the whites that nothing was happening. Agent Leeper, either not being informed that the local Indians wanted he out of the agency, or not caring, sent word he was returning. He arrived at Fort Cobb on the afternoon of October 23.

The Delaware troops were involved in one of the more controversial incidents in the Civil War, the sacking of Wichita Agency on October 23-24, 1862. In Union reports, this episode glowingly reported as a major Union victory, one that demonstrated Delaware "loyalty, daring, and hardihood." In the Confederate reports, the attack was presented as nothing more than a vicious massacre of other Indians and Confederate Indian Agency personnel, perpetuated by Indian marauders and deserters from the Union Army.

A Union Calvary of 196 men - 100 southern Kickapoo, 70 Delaware, and 26 Shawnee, left Fort Leavenworth during the 1st part of October 1862. Supplying their own horses and provisions, they had one objective - exact retribution upon Confederate officials and Confederate allied Indians at Wichita Agency. Although each Indian contingent had its own leadership, the Union Commander was Captain Ben Simons, a Delaware.

The 1st Kansas Home Guards were Creek and Seminole, 2nd Kansas Home Guards was made up of Delaware, Kickapoo, Osage, Shawnee, Seneca and some from the Five tribes. Some of the names in Captain Fall Leaf's Co. D, 2nd Kansas Home Guards were: Big Buffalo, Big beaver, Young Bear, Black Horse, Broken Knife, Yellow Leaf, Big Moccasin, Moonshine, Johnny Raccoon, Little Shanghai, Bear Skin, Soldier, Black Stump Jim Snake, Tea Nose, Black Wing and Whippoorwill, Lt. John Moss and Jim Ned.

With Union scouts and spies already infiltrated into the agency, they were able to take the agency by surprise late evening, October 23. In the attack, they reported they had killed agent Leeper and four other Confederate Indian agency personnel. However, Leeper had escaped by climbing from the rear window of his house and fleeing into the timber in his nightshirt. Old Towasi found him, gave him a horse and he fled to Texas. One Delaware was killed and one Shawnee wounded. They took the rebel flag, $1200.00 in Confederate money, 100 ponies, and Confederate correspondence, including original documents of Pike's treaties with the Nations of Indian Territory. Simon's forces then burned the agency buildings along with the five dead personnel.

At this time the Tonkawa were living along the Washita, south of the agency. Hearing the uproar, they abandoned most of their belongings and fled east. Before daylight, they halted and camped in a valley southeast of the site of Anadarko. They thought they were safe. Nevertheless, the other Indians relentlessly tracked them down and trapped them at noon in a black jack thicket along the Washita River. They killed approximately half the Tonkawa Nation, 137 people, including Chief Placido, 23 warriors and over 100 women and children. The few who escaped found refuge at Fort Arbuckle, and then went to Fort Griffin, Texas. The bones of their people lay bleaching for many years in what is now called Tonkawa Valley.

To the Historian, Annie Abel, "it was one of the bloodiest scenes ever enacted on the western plains" carried out by "good-for-nothing or vicious Indians."

Watie and Cooper retreated south of the Arkansas. The warmish fall weather of late November had turned cold and wet; they rode through cold and ice, then a pouring rain. Blunt marched back to northwest Arkansas and Scholfield withdrew the Second and Third Divisions from the region leaving Blunt and the First Division to hold the area.

On November 23, Colonel Jewell, with the Sixth Kansas Cavalry had scouted almost to Van Buren. He reported to Blunt at Lindsey's Prairie 30 miles north of Cane Hill, where Marmaduke and 7,000 troops were, that Watie and Hindman were preparing to leave Van Buren, heading north. Blunt took the initiative, forcing Marmaduke back from Cane Hill. On the 29th, Colonel Jewell was wounded and died. As Hindman advanced against Blunt, he sent for reinforcements from Brigadier General Frank J. Herron, who was camped at Wilson's Creek, some 116 miles from Cane Hill. He had about 8,000 men as opposed to Hindman's 15,000. To save Blunt, Herron would have to beat Hindman, only 60 miles away, to Cane Hill.

Watie's orders from Hindman on December 3, took him out of the fighting to come. He was sent to the Evansville area where they were to open a communications line for the Confederates, set pickets on the line road and occupy Dutch Mills. This would put him in the position to capture Federal supply trains, if the fighting forced them into the area of Dutch Mills.

On the 4th fourth, Watie and about 400 of his troops reached Dwight's Mission, and on the morning of the 5th, his scouts killed several Pin Indians. By night, the Cherokee Rifles reached Peyton's Springs about 4 miles from Evansville. The next morning they entered Evansville, finding that no Confederate pickets had been there for over a week, and the citizens did not know where the main Confederate Army was located.

Watie spent the day in the area and in the evening, knowing there were enemy troops at Cane Hill moved down Lee's Creek. On the morning of the 7th, the Rebels heard cannons in the distance, and returned to Peyton's Springs. Dutch Mills was in Rebel possession by the 8th and word sent to General Hindman. Maintaining communications was difficult, and Watie did not know just where Hindman was, so assumed he was near Cane Hill.

On December 6, Hindman had switched strategy and sent Marmaduke with the main body of troops against Herron, who was marching to reinforce Blunt. In this force were the men of Quantrill, Shelby, and Watie assigned to Hindman. Colonel Monroe's small force of Arkansas Cavalry remained to engage Blunt, until the main force returned.

Shelby and the cavalry rode out about 5:00 into the early dawn, with Quantrill's men, commanded in his absence by Dave Pool with Frank and Jesse James in the ranks. Quantrill's riders attacked Lt. Bunner's 6th and 7th Cavalry, sent them scurrying, while Colonel Emmet McDonald's Confederate Cavalry defeated the rest of the 6th and 7th Missouri, killing their commander, Major Eliphalet Bredett, and Captain William McKee. McDonald's and Quantrill's troops, scattered the First Arkansas Cavalry and captured the commissary wagons headed for Blunt; Shelby, riding in to take over the wagons, was surprised by a rallied company of the 7th Missouri and he, his staff and two artillery pieces were captured. About then, Confederates Major David Shanks and Pool with his men, and Colonels Young and Crump of McDonald's cavalry came down the road. Unexpectedly coming across the captured Shelby, the Rebel Cavalry then seized nearly 400 of the Missouri Cavalrymen and Shelby was free.

This was the fast start of the Confederates that morning. Hindman and his Indian allies were advancing toward the Prairie Grove Church where their advance stopped. 8,000 Rebels placed along a 2 mile along a ridge covered with heavy underbrush and trees waited to stop Herron's column. If he had continued his advance against the 6,000 exhausted troops with Herron, a Confederate victory would have been theirs.

Herron's troops, though exhausted, charged the Confederate line across Illinois Creek, repeatedly, but the Rebel Grays, despite a two-hour barrage by the Yankees, held and shot their enemies under cover of fences and houses. Shelby ambushed the 25th Illinois by apparently 'abandoning' four guns. When the Blue troops gathered around the "captured" guns, they opened up with concealed guns and blew them to pieces.

General Hindman started to give the order for attack when he realized something was wrong in the Confederate line. Colonel Adam's Arkansas conscripted unit had deserted, leaving only their officers on the field. Instead, Hindman ordered the line to hold. Moreover, they held, as wave after wave of Union blue surged forward.

Suddenly, artillery was falling on Herron's troops. He thought he was surrounded, and then the fire corrected as Blunt arrived with 3,000 cavalrymen, 20 guns, and infantry. Completely fooled at Cane Hill, Blunt thought he was facing the entire Confederate command instead of Colonel Monroe's skeleton Cavalry force, spread thin. The late morning gunfire from Prairie Grove alerted him to the decoy by the Southerners.

Confederate General Hindman's attempt to retake northwest Missouri met with defeat as Blunt was victorious at Prairie Grove December 7, 1862.

Blunt was impressed with the performances of the Indian Home Guards, so sent them on a special mission in late December. He ordered their commander Colonel William Phillips, back to Indian Territory to try to finish off Stand Watie and Colonel Cooper. Phillips was a Scot immigrant who had worked for the New York Times in Kansas in 1855. He was totally committed to the Union cause, a capable and dedicated officer.

Fort Davis

Phillips' force of 1,200 Home Guards, 2 companies of the Sixth Kansas Cavalry and a battery of 4 artillery pieces, taken at the battle of Fort Gibson, rode into Cherokee Nation on December 22. Moving southwest toward the Arkansas River, he found Fort Gibson nearly abandoned. A good size Confederate camp was across the river at Fort Davis that had been established by General Pike and named for the Confederate President. It is located just north of present day Muskogee, on a hill overlooking the Arkansas River Valley, opposite where the Grande and Verdigris Rivers enter.

The proud Confederate flag waved from the flagpole in the center of the fort in a crisp winter breeze, as Phillips' force approached on December 27. His artillery quickly blasted their holiday greetings. Skirmishers moved forward and after a brief exchange, the outnumbered Confederates abandoned Fort Davis to the Union. Phillips burned the post and followed Watie and Cooper into the Creek Nation, destroying the homes of the Southerners along the way.

As 1862 ended, the Confederate Warriors continued to elude their determined pursuers. Although they were out numbered and out gunned, they were not ready to surrender. Finally, Phillips withdrew to the Arkansas border for the winter, and Watie and Cooper set about to rally and re supply their commands.

A large portion of the Indians that had fled to Kansas for safety were moved to the Sac and Fox Agency. They included Creeks who had followed O-pothle-yohola, a few Euchee, Kickapoo, and Choctaws, about 225 Chickasaw and about 300 Cherokee. At Neosho Falls were about 750 refugee Seminoles. On the

Ottawa Reservation were the non-fighting Quapaws, Seneca, and Shawnee. Camped on the Verdigris and Fall Rivers were almost 2,000 refugees from the Leased District. These were mostly old people, women, and children, as the young men and warriors enlisted in the three Indian Home Guards Regiments.

Chapter Six

1863

On January 8, 1863, a new commander was appointed for the Southern troops in Indian Territory. Brigadier General William Steele had led a regiment in the Confederacy's ill-fated 1862 New Mexico campaign. The old Mexican War veteran was not pleased that he was given overall command in the Territory, as Colonel Cooper retained command of all Indian Troops. There developed a bitter rivalry between the two commanders that did not help the beleaguered Confederacy in the Territory. Steele assumed his command at Fort Smith, where he elected to maintain his headquarters and left Cooper the actual commander in the field, re-grouping his scattered forces of Indian and Texas troops.

With the Confederacy in the south part of the Territory, Cherokees of Union sympathies tried to establish control in the north. The Union Cherokee Council met in session in February in Tahlequah, under the protection of Phillips' troops and voted to void the treaty with the Confederacy. The council declared its allegiance to the United States, declared Stand Watie and his troops were outlaws and seized their property, abolished slavery in the tribe and voted Thomas Pegg in as Principal Chief to act in the absence of Chief Ross. For the rest of the war, there were two Cherokee governments, Union and Confederate.

In April, Blunt ordered Phillips to start moving the Indian refugees back into Indian Territory. The large number that had spent the winter at Neosho, Missouri was in bad shape. Many had died due to a small pox outbreak. About 1,000 started the long trek with Phillips' 3,000 troops back to Indian Territory.

After the command passed into the Cherokee Nation, the physical looks of the country changed with every mile. It was less broken and more inviting and seemed better adapted to agricultural and grazing than Arkansas. The Indians showed good judgment in wanting to get back to their own country.

The Indian wagon train with the families arrived at Park Hill on the ninth, escorted by the Union Warriors. It had been on the trail for ten days. It was about a mile long, using every type vehicle, on some days traveling only three or four miles. Many of the families left to return to what remained of their homes in the Cherokee and Creek Nations. Since the season was still early, there was time to get crops put in with the seeds they brought.

Phillips camped at Park Hill and sent the Second Home Guard and a detachment of the Sixth Kansas cavalry to scout for the enemy. They found Watie had left a small Rebel force at Fort Gibson. The Union attacked and literally drove the small force into the Grande River to swim for their lives. On April 13, Phillips rode into Fort Gibson followed by the Army's supply wagons and hundreds of Union Creeks and Seminoles, still homeless because their lands were in the tight grip of the Confederacy.

Fort Gibson

The First, Second and Third Indian Home Guards, four companies of Kansas cavalry and Hopkins battery, aggregating three thousand one hundred fifty men occupied Ft. Gibson April 8, 1863. They threw up some earthworks above the site of the old post and called it Fort Blount in honor of Major General James G. Blunt, USA, then, in command of Kansas and Indian Territory.

Fort Gibson was a good defensive position, built on a bluff overlooking the Grand River, near the intersection of the two main arteries of travel for trade in the Territory, the Arkansas River, and the Texas Road. The fort had a couple of log blockhouses, two large stone buildings and several small wood frame houses. Soon after taking the fort, Phillips renamed it Fort Blunt, but the name did not catch on, as it was still referred to as Fort Gibson. The post was a key stronghold but its major disadvantage was, the supply base at Fort Scott was 160 miles away. Half his force would have to patrol to protect the line of communications and supply.

The Southern forces of the Cherokee sent word that the Legislature was meeting April 25 at Webber's Falls for the election of a Principle Chief of the Cherokee and the military situation. Stand Watie was made chairman by acclamation and requested to state the reason for the meeting. The Colonel gracefully accepted the honor of selection to preside. He thanked everyone then spoke:

"Leaders and Councilors of the Cherokee People:

This meeting has been called for the purpose of talking over the questions to be submitted to the Legislative council tomorrow, the most important of which are the election of principle chief and the military situation. You know I am a candidate for principle chief and will be satisfied to leave that matter in the hands of my friends. The old chief, John Ross, you know, has gone over to the enemy after pledging his allegiance to the South, and is now living in the North with the Yankees, and is recognized by them as an abolitionist in full fellowship."

"In regard to the military situation, I can speak of it only with a heavy heart, for evil times have come upon our country. Many of our people have fled their homes and living among the Indians south of us, and some in Texas, homeless and destitute. The

Confederates in the Indian Country and in Western Arkansas have had no substantial success since the Federal forces invaded and occupied our country last summer. Recently they have occupied Fort Gibson with several thousand Indians and a contingent of white soldiers, and, we are informed, with the determination of making the occupation permanent, having commenced fortifying it. Disaster upon disaster has followed the Confederate arms in the Cherokee country and near its borders, commencing with the battle of Pea Ridge, then Locust Grove, Newtonia, Old Fort Wayne, Cane Hill, Prairie Grove, Van Buren, and recently as I have stated, the Federal occupation of fort Gibson. These reverses and disasters following each other in rapid succession without any important successes to our credit are very depressing to all of us and discouraging and lower the morale of our troops everywhere, particularly those operating in Indian country. And I know it is distressing to everyone here to realize that we shall be obliged to hold our legislative council outside the limits of our own country."

"I am informed by higher Confederate authorities that the Confederate forces operating in the Indian country will not likely be materially strengthened until the larger Federal forces under General Grant operating against Vicksburg shall determine the fate of that strong position. We hope that the Confederate commanders will be able to defeat and drive back the Federal forces of Grant and throw a powerful Confederate army into Arkansas under aggressive leaders, and thus, relieve our present uncertain situation. "

"But, we must remember that the Federal forces of Missouri, Arkansas and Kansas have been heavily drawn upon to strengthen the forces operating against Vicksburg, and that we should be able very soon with the assistance of the Texas regiments we have had with us, and General Cabell's brigade in Western Arkansas, to attack and capture or drive out the Federal force of Indians and small contingent of white soldiers occupying Fort Gibson, or capture or destroy their supply trains and starve them into surrendering by making their position untenable."

General Steele, commanding the Department of the Indian Territory, and General Cooper, commanding the Confederate forces in the field, are collecting supplies at North Fork, Perryville and Boggy Depot, and reorganizing our forces for a vigorous campaign. These forces will be largely superior in number to the Federal forces occupying Fort Gibson, and we must arouse ourselves in the determination to attack, capture or destroy, or by interrupting their communication with the North and cutting off their supplies, starve them into surrendering. Our successful operations in the regions in this region would hearten Confederate forces in other quarters. I believe that the time is near at hand when the tide of success is due to return to the Confederate arms when we shall be able to drive the Federal forces out of our country, which will enable our people, many now exiles, to return home".

When word came to Phillips that a sizable force of Confederates were gathered at Webber's Fall, 25 miles south, he took 600 men, Indian troops from the three Home Guard and a battalion of 6th Kansas Cavalry to attack. They crossed the Arkansas River and marched all night down the south side. The surprise attack at dawn on April 25 came as the Confederate Council was about to go into session. Some of Watie's men did not have time to dress; they fled in the direction of North Fork and Fort Smith, leaving their camp and supplies in the hands of the Federal forces. The newly appointed principal chief, Stand Watie, tried to rally his men, but it was not successful, with 15 Rebels killed, as many wounded and two Yankees killed and ten wounded. They were pursued only a short distance because of the worn condition of the men and animals from the forced night march, besides the Arkansas was rising and was already at the danger point to ford at Webber's Falls. The captured equipment and supplies were destroyed.

The most serious loss to the Federals was the death of Dr. Rufus Gilpatrick, an advisory agent to the Government who had accompanied the Indian Brigade. After the action was over, an Indian woman summoned him to tend a wounded Indian soldier about one hundred yards away. While attending the wound, he was shot by a party of Southern Indians who came out of the cane. He was taken back and buried at Fort Gibson with military honors.

On May 15, 1863, an odd clash took place north of the Cherokee Nation on the Osage Reservation in Kansas. A small party of Osage encountered a column of blue coats crossing their land, heading toward the northwest. Though a normal sight, the Osage did not recognize these troopers. The troopers were nervous in answering the Osage's questions, with vague answers. The Indians suggested they all ride together to the nearby army post, but the soldiers refused and started to ride away. When the Osage tried to stop them, a shot rang out and a tribesman fell from his pony.

Out numbered the Osage galloped away to their camp with the news. Soon about 200 Osage, led by Hard Rope followed the white men's trail and caught up with them on the prairie near present Independence, Kansas. A hard fought skirmish ensued; ammo expended the troopers fought hand to hand with the Osage, who swarmed like angry bees. One by one, the soldiers fell on the bloody sandbar, where they had made their last stand. They were stripped of their uniforms and equipment, scalped, then scalped and beheaded.

Later, the Osage informed the army and a detachment of the Ninth Kansas sent to the scene found several articles of Confederate origin. They then swung by Hard Rope's village and he gave their commander some water-stained documents found in the clothes of the soldiers. These turned out to be official Confederate communiqués that revealed a special task force of 20 Confederate officers, led by Colonel Charles Harrison, had been ordered by Major General Theophilus Holmes to ride west on a mission to incite the plains tribes to wage war on the settlers in Kansas and Nebraska.

They were to obtain the help of white southern sympathizers. They would promise weapons and ammunition to the plains tribes for their help. The purpose was to draw Union troops away from Missouri and Arkansas. The 9th Kansas found only 18 bodies, two Southern officers, Colonel Warner Lewis and John Rafferty, had managed to escape and make it back to friendly territory.

Phillips was growing concerned about his precarious position at Fort Gibson. Rebel forces under Cooper had regrouped and reinforced by new regiments of Texas cavalry and a battery of three mountain howitzers. Cooper's forces of 5,000 now outnumbered Phillips troops at Gibson. The Rebel forces marched north and set up camp about five miles south of the post on the opposite side of the Arkansas River under cover of the trees in the valley. Confederate troops in Arkansas under Brigadier General William Cabel had pressured Federal troops to withdraw from their base near Fayetteville. If the two forces joined, Phillips could not hold the fort very long. He sent urgent requests for reinforcement to General Blunt.

For weeks, the pickets on both sides of the river exchanged fire, with light casualties. Eventually they became less hostile to each other and occasionally met on a sand bar in the river to exchange items. It was a standoff for both sides. Cooper realized during this time the Union force would graze their off duty cavalry horses all day within a two or three miles radius of the fort.

Cooper felt confident enough to order out a detachment to turn the Union horses into Rebel horses. During the night of May 19, five regiments of Confederates crossed the river and positioned themselves for the raid. About 9:00, they dashed from cover near the herd, quickly over ran the pickets and herders, and gathered the horses. Forming a skirmish line, they advanced on the fort. Some of the herders had made it back to raise the alarm. Bugles sounded and the Yankee troopers ran to their posts. Union Cavalry galloped out to meet the Rebels, skirmished briefly, and then fell back to the shelter of the fort's walls.

Soon 2,000 troops manned the trenches and Phillips advanced with two battalions of the Home Guards on foot, a section of the 3rd Kansas Light Artillery. The two forces clashed about a mile from the fort. With help from the Union cavalry, Phillips drove Cooper's forces back, but he was unable to recapture all his horses. Union casualties were 20 killed, 20 wounded; Confederate losses were uncertain, likely about the same. If Cooper had advanced his whole force that day, he could have retaken Fort Gibson for the Confederacy.

First Cabin Creek

The Federals at Fort Gibson had to solve a serious problem to get enough supplies to hold their position. Possibly as many as 15,000 Indian refugees had followed the Union troops into Indian Territory. After two devastating winters in Kansas, the refugees wanted to return home and reclaim their homes. Finding stock and supplies in the re-occupied territory was out of the question. Foraging raids by both sides had stripped the country. They would return to nothing.

In response to Phillips pleas for reinforcements and supplies, Blunt sent a strong force south escorting a wagon train heavy with food, ammunition, and equipment. The relief force consisted of six companies of the Second Colorado Regiment, one company of the Third Wisconsin Cavalry, a company each from the Ninth and 14th Kansas cavalry and a section of the 2nd Kansas artillery under command of Lt. Colonel Theodore Dodd. When the wagon train arrived at Baxter Springs, Kansas, about 80 miles north of the fort, it added additional troops.

Among them, a newly formed First Kansas Colored Infantry under Colonel James M. Williams. A detachment of several hundred from Fort Gibson arrived to escort the train to the safety of the fort. Major John Foreman led elements of the three Indian Home Guards and the Sixth Kansas Cavalry. Blunt knew if the train fell, Fort Gibson would be next. Colonel Phillips sent 600 of his troops to reinforce the train. Watie and Cooper knew that the rations at Fort Gibson had been reduced to fresh beef, salt, rice, and wheat and sickness from the diet switch was sweeping the Union camp.

Although Cabin Creek was an unimpressive stream in 1862, the road crossing it was a very important artery of travel. It was a much used wagon road south, known under several names, Military Road, Texas Road, Immigrant Road, or Osage Trail, prior to the war. There was a thriving community at the Cabin

Creek crossing, with areas cleared for farms and open pastures for livestock. The road carried freight from Fort Scott Kansas to Forts Gibson in Indian Territory, and Smith in Arkansas. At the Kansas line the Military Road forked, with the west trail running south along the west bank of the Grand River and the east trail to Fort Gibson.

As the long column of troops and 300 wagons made its way down the "Military Road" that connected Fort Scott and Fort Gibson, Confederate scouts kept Colonel Stand Watie informed of its progress. This road had been a target many times, as Rebels attacked the supply trains. Anything that moved on the road was subject to attacks anywhere. Watie, with his reinforced command, planned to attack the Union column at the ford on Cabin Creek in now far south Craig County. On June 26, as the train crossed the Grand River, Union scouts ahead came upon tracks of many horses. Carefully following the tracks, they found a large force of Confederate Indians and Texans at the ford. The troops were seen and fired upon, as they raced back to the wagons with a couple of prisoners they happened to capture.

After questioning, the Union found out that Stand Watie and more than 2,000 men were waiting at the ford for them. They also learned General Cabell was in the area, but because of high water, he was cut off from Watie. Due to the heavy rains and muddy road, the train was slow in arriving at the ford, which gave the Union command time to plan for it. High water made the ford impassable. The Federals had good reason to fear Watie. He was an inspiring leader, known for his hit and run tactics!

On July 1, 1863, the wagon train rumbled toward the crossing. The Military Road at that time crossed Cabin Creek about three miles above where it empties into the Grand River. There was a strip of timber and brush along the creek, above and below the ford, nearly two miles wide. North of the ford, the heights overlooked the strip of timber and the country for several miles south. The Southern forces were occupying a strong position, from which it would not be easy to remove them. They occupied the timber along the south bank above and below the ford for a mile. Confederate pickets were scattered along the north bank, well positioned to give an advance warning of the train's arrival.

The wagons circled on the prairie about two miles from the ford. Leaving the Sixth Kansas to guard them, the Union moved into battle formation As the Confederates, concealed in the brush in rifle pits on the opposite side of the creek watched. It was already hot and humid that July 2 morning, promising to be a scorcher. The U.S. Army officers gave their commands and the troops started nervously forward under sporadic gunfire from snipers across the creek. The Second Kansas artillery opened fire on the brush lining the south bank of Cabin Creek, hoping to soften the Rebels' position before charging. Union artillery was placed, two 6-pounders to the extreme left of the line, one 12-pounder howitzer and one "mountain rifle" in the center, directly in front and about 200 yards from the Rebel position, and the last piece, a 12 pounder howitzer on the Federal right.

For more than 30 minutes, artillery shells churned the ground and splintered trees as the Confederate troop hugged the ground in their rifle pits. Believing the Rebels had scattered with the artillery, Major Foreman waved his saber aloft and charged with a company of mounted Indian troopers. Furiously, they charged across the rain-swollen creek, water up to their horses bellies, struggling to the opposite shore, screaming defiantly.

The Rebels rose from their pits and began blasting away at the blue-clad warriors. Blood mingled with the muddy water as men and horses struggled, trying to make their way back to Union lines, seriously wounding Major Foreman. Watie's Cherokees had not fallen back as believed. Seeing Foreman fall, the advance moved back to their former positions. The Federal infantry had moved into position to cover the Ninth Cavalry charge. The Federals opened fire again with the howitzers for about another twenty minutes. Clouds of gun smoke rolled across the creek as the stubborn Kansans gained a foothold on the muddy creek bank in front of the Confederate rifles. Colonel Williams 1st Kansas Colored Infantry crossed waist deep creek, holding their rifles and cartridge boxes overhead to keep them dry, and formed a battle line on the other side in a hail of rifles and shotguns. The former slaves followed their white colonel through the brush, over running the rifle pits in a mad dash through the woods.

Watie stubbornly refused to give up his tactical position, although out gunned and out numbered. Williams, knowing he had to force the crossing and get the supplies to Fort Gibson, had to keep the initiative and drive Watie away. He ordered two companies of cavalry under Captain Stewart to position on his right to prevent any flank movement and the company commanded by Lieutenant Philbrick to charge the advance line of the Confederates, penetrate, and if possible find out their strength and position. Philbrick charged head-on into Watie's line, broke through, and put them to flight.

Watie's men tried to regroup about a quarter mile away, but again broke as the Yankees pushed forward. Many of the Confederates retreated to the Grand River and drowned along with their horses in swift swollen river. Exact figures are unknown of the

Southern losses at Cabin Creek, but Union estimates were about 50 killed and 50 wounded, Union casualties at three dead and 30 wounded. Bodies of the dead soldiers and horses could be seen floating down the river past Fort Gibson.

Williams estimated Watie's strength at about 1,600 to 1,800 consisting of the Cherokee and Creek Regiments and about 600 troopers from the 27th and 29th Texas Cavalry Regiments in his report.To the cheers of the half-starved men, the badly needed supplies and reinforcements finally reached Fort Gibson on July 5, good news for Phillips and his hungry troops. The Battle at Cabin Creek was one of the first actions of the war where black troops fought alongside white troops, proving it was possible and was a winning combination. At the time of this battle, across the country to the east, Union and Confederate Armies faced each other at Gettysburg, and on the Mississippi, the siege of Vicksburg was nearing its end. The summer of 1863, was destined to be the turning point of the War.

When word of the fight at Cabin Creek reached General Blunt, he led an additional force from Fort Scott to Fort Blunt (Gibson). They arrived on July 11, after a forced march. He assumed command of the fort, which had now about 3,000 troops with 12 artillery pieces.

Scouts soon brought word that General Cabell was marching from Fort Smith with 3,000 men and artillery to meet Colonel Cooper and his force of 6,000 troops and four artillery pieces, at his camp 25 miles south of Fort Gibson at Honey Springs. They would make an all out effort to retake Fort Gibson and drive the Union from Indian Territory. Blunt was determined he would defeat Watie and Cooper before the Arkansas troops arrived.

Honey Springs

The Confederate camp and supply depot at Honey Springs, 18 miles below Fort Gibson, near the site of present day Muskogee in the Creek Nation, consisted of a frame commissary building, a log hospital, several brush arbors, and hundreds of tents. Several springs provided fresh water. By July 1863, it was the most important Confederate installation in Indian Territory. It also became the primary objective for General Blunt, who intended to take it before General Cabell could reinforce Cooper. At midnight on July 15, Blunt rode out of Fort Gibson; it was time for a decisive, major battle in Indian Territory. This clash would determine the outcome of the war and the fate of the people in this area. The day of reckoning was at hand.

Blunt's force crossed the swollen Arkansas River on rafts. Several Indian troops drowned when they tried to swim across. By 10:00 that evening, his forces were across the river and headed for Elk Creek and Honey Springs. About midnight a skirmish occurred near Chimney Mountain between the Union leads and Confederate scouts, during a rain shower. The Southern soldiers noticed a serious problem that could strongly influence the upcoming battle; some of the gunpowder absorbed moisture from the wet weather and would not fire.

On July 17, when the Union forces came into sight, the Confederate troops were ready. The 20th Texas, dismounted cavalry, supported the battery in front, 9th Texas Cavalry and the Fifth Partisan Rangers formed the center. Unfortunately, Stand Watie was on detached service at Webber's Falls and Colonel Adair was ill, leaving command to Major Thompson of the First Cherokee and Lt. Colonel Bell, the Second Cherokee. These units made up the right wing. Colonel

Daniel N. McIntosh with his First and Second Creek Regiments led the left wing. The Choctaw and Chickasaw Regiments and two squadrons of Texas Cavalry made up the reserves.

Unfortunately, the powder supply was low-grade cheap Mexican gunpowder, which was useless because of the rains. This was on top of another serious problem - they were badly outgunned by Blunt's forces. Although they outnumbered the Union by two to one, many of the Confederate Indian troops were without adequate weapons. The Union army had standard long-range Springfield rifles, up-to-date breech loading rifles, and pistols. Cooper's troops had a wide variety, many captured Federal guns, and civilian firearms, including shotguns, which were good only at short range. Cooper had four light artillery pieces, three mountain howitzers and a smaller field piece called a "mountain rifle." Only 18 of these existed, and somehow one had made it out into Indian Territory.

On the other hand, Blunt had twelve artillery pieces, six big "Napoleon" cannon designed to fire 12-pound shells, two large model 1841 field guns that fired 6-pound shells and four mountain howitzers.

The battle of Honey Springs began about daylight on July 17, near the site of present day community of Rentiesville, along the eastern border of the old Creek Nation. The Sixth Kansas charged about 500 Confederate Cavalrymen positioned along the Texas Road. The 6th drove the Rebels south in a flurry of pistol fire. About 8:00 Blunt's forces found Cooper's Rebels ready for action along a defensive line on the north side of Elk Creek. Blunt halted his troops just out of range for a brief rest, as they had marched all night to reach here. Blunt and his staff rode forward some to view the positions of the enemy. They soon began drawing shots from the Confederate sharpshooters and took cover after one of the staff was shot from his saddle.

This day was hot and humid, also, the rain showers making the humidity climb. Another cloudburst cooled the hot, sweaty troops from both sides, and the Yankees filled their canteens from the puddles on the road. About 9:30, Blunt formed his troops into two columns. He assigned Colonel William R. Judson, of the 6th Kansas, the cavalry brigade of the 2nd Colorado, 1st Indian Home Guard, and the 6th Kansas on the west side of the road. Colonel William Phillips led the Second Indian Home Guard, Third Wisconsin, and Colonel James Williams' First Kansas Colored Infantry. Drums rolled, flags unfurled and the Union marched south toward Elk Creek, where the nervous Rebels waited. About a quarter mile away, the Union formed battle lines. Facing them, from the woods, were Cooper's ragged troops, with their rifles, shotguns, bayonets, and Bowie knives. Cooper faced the Yankees with two Cherokee regiments (Watie going to Webber's Falls as a diversion), two Creek Regiments of Colonel Daniel McIntosh, the 20th and 29th Texas Cavalry Regiments, the Fifth Texas Partisan Rangers, Tandy's First and Second Choctaw and Chickasaw Mounted Rifles and four-gun artillery under Captain R. W. Lee.

About 10:00 artillery from both sides started blasting away for more than an hour. Captain Lee fired the first volley and gave the Union guns a good battle, scoring a direct hit on one of the Union's big Napoleon cannons, killing an artillery sergeant, a private and four horses in the explosion. Captains Edward Smith and Henry Hopkins concentrated the fire of the Union guns soon hit a Confederate howitzer, killing the crew and horses. The Rebel's accurate little Mountain Rifle, landed shells on the high ground beyond the battle line, killing one of Blunt's aides and narrowly missing Captain Smith as he direct fire from his artillery.

Union Infantry and dismounted cavalry moved forward and opened fire on the Confederate position in the brush along Elk creek. For more than two hours, lead flew from both sides. The Rebels realized they had more numbers and attempted a flanking move on the left, only to be met and hurled back by C, F, and H companies of the Sixth Kansas with their Sharps rifles.

The Indian Home Guards became overly enthusiastic and advanced far out in front, exposed to "friendly fire." The Federals had to stop firing until they could fall back to their position. This created a false impression to the dismounted 29th Texas, who believed the Union force was about to break. They advanced to within about 25 feet of the First Kansas Colored Infantry, who lay hidden in the smoke and tall grass. They leveled a direct fire at the Texans, resulting with the first line completely destroyed.

A second volley tore into their ranks, causing the Texans to retreat. As the Texans retreated, the complete defense line of the Confederates collapsed. Cooper realized he had no hope of holding the line at this point and ordered the artillery to pull back across the bridge on Elk Creek. Many Texas troopers died defending the bridge long enough for the heavy artillery to pull across the bridge.

Cooper's troops pulled back down the Texas Road to Honey Springs camp. There Colonel Walker's Choctaw and Chickasaw and two squadrons of Texas Cavalry drew a new defensive line, delaying the Yankees long enough to save the main portion of the Rebel army, including artillery and supply wagons. The buildings and supplies were set on fire by the retreating Confederates, but Blunt's forces arrived in time to save large amounts of bacon, flour, sorghum, and salt.

By 2:00, the battle was over and Cooper's broken demoralized army moved east as a steady rain began to fall. Two hours later, he met Cabell's 3,000 troops, too late to save the Southern Cause in Indian Territory. Together the tow forces moved south to the Canadian River. Despite the heavy gunfire, the casualties had been light. Cooper's losses were 134 killed and wounded, 47 captured. Blunt's casualties were 17 killed and 60 wounded.

The Battle of Honey Springs or Elk Creek marked the end of large-scale Confederate military resistance in the Territory. Never again would the Confederates be able to gather a full size army to fight the Union. Although the war was to last two more years, the South had lost the war when the last Confederate soldier fell on the bridge over Elk Creek, that hot wet, July day. This battle has been referred to as the "Gettysburg of Indian Territory."

General Cooper re-crossed the Canadian River into the Creek Nation on July 23, 1863, intending to confront Blunt again, but was defeated once more. Cooper's troops retired south by way of the main public road leading to Texas. By September, Union forces controlled the area north of the Canadian and Arkansas Rivers, preparing for a push south to the Red River.

After the battle at Honey Springs, Blunt marched his troops back to Fort Gibson to re-supply. While he had been gone, more troops had arrived raising his force to more than 4.500. News also arrived of Cabell and Cooper's forces linking up and he was determined to keep the pressure on until the Confederacy was destroyed in the Territory. In addition, General William Steele had arrived at the Confederate camp to take command of the Rebel army, much to the displeasure of General Cooper.

In the evening of August 22, General Blunt took his troops out again, marching south toward the

Confederate camp on the Canadian River. They marched 60 miles in 48 hours, only to find the camp abandoned. One of the most fateful and important decisions had been made by the Confederate commanders; they split their troops up, ending the possibility of another decisive strategically important battles in the Territory. Cabell had marched back to Arkansas, Steele and Cooper had pulled farther south toward Perryville, and McIntosh's Creeks moved west toward the headwaters of the Canadian. Now began a deadly game of cat and mouse between the well-armed Federals and the ragged confederate troops. All victories and defeats would be short lived and fleeting, as the morning mists on the river.

Perryville, IT

Blunt continued on south and on August 26, his scouts brought word that Steele, Cooper, and Watie were only 25 miles ahead of him. He moved his troops out to pursue. Before long, the front of the Union forces came upon the rear guard of the Confederates. Blunt's Indian troops moved through the brush and when contact was made with the Confederates, Union cavalry was ordered forward to push the Rebels farther. Blunt stayed on their trail all day and about 8:00 reached the vicinity of Perryville.

The Rebel commanders decided to make a stand and placed two howitzers on the road leading into town, and their troops behind makeshift barricades. The Sixth Cavalry dismounted and took positions along the sides of the road, and advanced firing their deadly Sharps. The outnumbered Confederates answered with a variety of weapons from behind their pitiful barricades. When the Federal artillery opened up, the Rebel Warriors fled into the darkness, heading for the

Red River. Since Perryville was a supply depot, Blunt loaded all they could carry and burned the rest.

The next morning, Blunt divided his forces, sending Colonel Judson with the 1st Indian Regiment, 2nd Colorado, and 6th Kansas west in the Territory after McIntosh's Creeks. He headed off to Arkansas. During Judson's hard riding pursuit, McIntosh lost more of his troops to desertion, leaving him with only about 150 troops. Judson had destroyed the Creek forces with firing a shot and headed back to Fort Gibson without losing a man. Soon the starving, ragged deserters arrived at Fort Gibson, declaring their loyalty to the United States and begging for food.

The refugee Indians in all locations were dissatisfied. They were tired of changed habits of life, scarce food, and were homesick. The Seminoles at Neosho Falls were more comfortable than most of the refugees, suffering less. Their old chief, Billy Bowleggs, was away at Camp Bentonville, but he wrote sadly of his own hope to return to the country he had not set foot in since the war began. The country was dear to him, not only because it held the bones of his ancestors, but, because it was "home." Home meant a reunion with his family.

He envied the Cherokee soldiers who were now in close touch with their women and children. He admitted there was great confusion in the Territory; but he had noticed empty houses there, deserted, in which he felt his people could find shelter. This fueled the people and they begged the Great Father to send them back. They would go that very fall, no matter what lay in their way. A return in the autumn or winter would allow them to gather cattle and hogs to furnish meat, and at the same time prepare their fields for a spring crop.

The Indian Agent, Snow, doubted they would be able to maintain themselves in their devastated country during the winter, but that did not deter them. They had known scarcity of food that past winter in Kansas and might fare better farther south. Anyway, they could burn green wood there, as they were not allowed to on the White man's land.

"Billy Bowleggs, Fos-huchee-ha-jo, No-ko-so-lo-chee, Koch-e-me-ko to Oak-to-ha and Pas-co-fa:
We have got a letter from Billy Bowleggs and others....and from what we hear in this letter we think we can go home with safety. We know it will be impossible for the government to haul provisions all the way down there for us. We have taken all this into consideration. We know we will live hard this winter, but we want to go home on our own land. We must be there this fall if we expect to plant in the spring. Corn must be put in there in March. Fences must be built, houses repaired, farms improved and this must all be done before we can expect to raise a crop."

"We are here on the white man's land – we cannot cut green wood to burn and when we got word from Billy Bowleggs that we can get in our own country, we are anxious to go where we can burn green wood as we please. And we would ask you to help us move down before cold weather sets in. Our dear Father, if you can only get wagons, we want you to get all you can to help us back to our homes. ...And if you can't help us then we will try what we can do in moving ourselves. We expect that the rebels have destroyed all our property, but we think if we can get to our Brothers the Cherokee we could get enough of them to live on, until we could raise something for ourselves. "

(Pas-ko-ffa, Seminole; Tus-ta-nuk-e-mantha, Creek; Robert Smith, Cherokee; Lewis, Chickasaw; to Wm. P. Dole, dated Neosho Falls, KS, September 14, 1863)

The homesickness of the refugees was due to many causes, a main one being the forced change of living habits. Their homes in Indian Territory were comfortable and warm. They had lived in modern homes, had plenty of fruit, vegetables and meat. In Kansas, they lived in cast off army tents, not enough to protect them from the weather, their clothes were threadbare, their bodies undernourished due to scarcity of food. The mortality rate was appalling.

They were also apprehensive of the charges against their account, because, from long experience, they had no illusions as to the white man's generosity. They had heard the whisperings about graft. They knew they had outstayed their welcome in Kansas and that, the citizens were not profiting from the relief money, wanted them gone. On the Ottawa Reservation and to some extent on the Sac and Fox, their Indian hosts were no longer sympathetic.

The Creeks however were afraid to venture back home, until they received assurances their enemies had been cleaned out. Military protection would have to be a provision and it would have to extend farther than Fort Gibson, north, and south of the Arkansas River. That river needed to be opened for navigation. Once safe, the Indians would haul their own supplies; but they wanted more than the Cherokee country cleared and protected. The Chickasaws, for instance, could not go back until Forts Washita and Arbuckle were seized and garrisoned. A small incompetent force in Indian Territory was worse than none at all. It simply invited attack.

The Confederate troops in the Territory were so demoralized and out of supplies that for the most part they were not an effective fighting force any more, with one exception----Stand Watie's Cherokee Mounted Rifles! Watie had become a master of guerrilla tactics - hit and run attacks against the Yankees, keeping his men supplied with captured Union gear, weapons, ammunition and food, that the Southern Cause still lived. This charismatic leader, with his little victories in numerous skirmishes with the Union, kept the little spark of rebellion alive in the hearts of the Southerners. To most Indians and many whites in the Territory, Stand Watie became the symbol of fury and defiance for the Cause of the South.

Unfortunately, Watie's type of leadership was not common among the Confederates commanders in the Territory. Many Southern units, not just the Indian troops, chose their own leaders. Most times these leaders were not disciplinarian combat leaders. Cooper had often complained that his troops would go home whenever they wished, being absent for long times. Union troops were led by appointed white officers and not concerned with pleasing their troops, just making sure they were fed and equipped properly to be in good fighting condition.

As fall and winter, 1863 approached, the merciless guerilla war continued, Watie's raids grew more frequent, and the Union soldiers lost patience with the civilians in the area. Cavalry units on both sides "requisitioned" nearly every horse they saw, along with pigs, chickens, and cattle for food for the troops. An honest Union officer, Major Preston Plumb, discovered in the fall of 1863, that a group of cattle dealers was paying the Osage $2.00 a head, to steal cattle in the Territory and bring them back to Kansas. The dealers would then sell the cattle to the army at much higher prices. Several army officers and prominent citizens were involved in the cattle-rustling scheme that Plumb broke up. The charges were discreetly dropped.

Along with the livestock, the soldiers ate or destroyed the crops on the farms. With no livestock or crops, many families were without food. Nearly 18,000

Southern Cherokees and Creeks fled south to the Choctaw and Chickasaw lands to find food and shelter and escape the Federals. Now the Confederates found themselves burdened with thousands of hungry, homeless, Indians, camped near Confederate posts on the Red River. .

The weather got colder as the refugees tried to prepare for what would be a miserable winter. Food and shelter were scarce. The Choctaw and Chickasaw did what they could to help, sharing what little food and shelter they had. The winter looked very bleak. Steele and Cooper, still not getting along, consulted their maps and supply lists to see if they could come up with a plan to re-take Fort Gibson. Even with the arrival of Colonel Richard M. Gano and 1,000 more troops, Steele still was not confident enough he had the strength to take the fort. Instead, he sent Watie on another series of raids.

In October and November, Watie raided north. He outflanked the Union lines around Fort Gibson and attacked the Union Cherokee at Tahlequah where he burned the capitol buildings on October 28 and on the following day, he burned Chief Ross' house at Park Hill. The following month he rode out of Indian Territory skirmishing with the Union in southwest Missouri.

As 1863 grew to a close, General Steel frustrated with what he saw as a no win situation and mentally exhausted by the infighting with Cooper and Watie, requested to be relieved of duty in Indian Territory. On December 11, he received his new orders and in the same packet, assigning a new commander, again overlooking General Douglas and bringing in another outsider. The war was becoming very tiring for Cooper and many others.

In December 1863, the new commander appointed for the Confederate forces in Indian Territory was Gen. Samuel B. Maxey, a veteran of the

Army of Tennessee. Maxey was dedicated to the Southern Cause and planned a more aggressive campaign than his predecessor. He began drilling and supplying his men for action.

Chapter 7

1863

There was a Grand Council of the Southern factions of the Five Civilized Tribes held February 1 at Armstrong Academy, Choctaw Nation. The purpose of the meeting was to establish peace and friendship between all the tribes and get them to pledge allegiance to the Confederacy and battle tactics. Watie's men had moved the Federals beyond the Choctaw Nation borders and Confederate officials assured them the Stars and Bars would stay over their Nation. General Maxey, commander of the Southern forces in Indian Territory had high respect for the Confederate leaders, and felt that the Five Nations were aristocracies, and in them, the educated minorities took the lead. Moty Kinnard, the Creek leader was quite impressed. He was invited to address the council:

"Chiefs and Leaders of the Indian Nations:
I have been assigned by the Confederate Government to the command of the Confederate forces in the District of Indian Territory; I salute you as your friend and brother in the struggle in which we are mutually engaged. I beg to assure you that I shall do everything in my power for the happiness and welfare of your people, and to protect and restore them to their homes. But first we must prepare ourselves for the work before us and drive out the invaders who have driven your non-combatant people from their homes and taken or destroyed their property."

"Before I took command of the Confederate forces in this District, they had been defeated so many times and retired so often that they could not have retired any further south without crossing Red River into Texas. Your troops did not have the confidence in their commander essential to successful operations. We must not retire another step; we must advance and make the enemy retire. Let us advance, and let "advance" be our watch word all along the line; we can do it; we must do it."

"General Smith, commanding the Trans-Mississippi Department, has promised to support me with troops and supplies. We confidently believe that his forces will recapture Little Rock, and we must drive the Federal white and Negro troops from Fort Smith, and the renegade Indians and white troops from Fort Gibson and recapture and occupy those places and hold the Arkansas River until we shall be ready to advance to the northern part of the Indian country."

"And finally, let me appeal to you, to advise all your people, except your warriors, who have left their homes to return and raise crops, part of which we will need for our forces, and for which we will pay you fair prices. You shall soon see the effect of my active, aggressive policy. I shall lose no time in setting my forces in operation; I promise to drive in the enemy outposts at Waldron and at points in the Choctaw Nation. I want your full cooperation in carrying out all movements assigned in my plans of ridding your country of the enemy who have insolently trampled upon your rights. We hope to win the war this year; we hear that the enemy people at home are tired of the war to conquer the South and will not support war measures with men and money much longer."

Before Maxey got his forces reorganized, however, Col. William Phillips set out from Fort Gibson, on February 1, with about 1500 Cavalry troopers on a "scorched earth" march to show the power and wraith of the Federal army and the futility of opposing it. Phillip's forces consisted of some of the

First, Third Home Guards, and a portion of the 14th Kansas.

In early January, President Lincoln had written a proclamation in each Indian language, in which he offered pardons to any Indians willing to stop fighting and support the Union. Phillips decided to deliver this in person to tribal leaders along the way, such as this letter to John Jumper, with his own proclamation added:

In essence, his letter stated, "The Great Government of the United States will soon crush all enemies. Let me know if you want to be among them." He told his men; "Those who are still in arms are Rebels and should die. Do not kill a prisoner after he has surrendered. But I do not ask you to take prisoners. I do ask that you make your footsteps severe and terrible".

Phillips rode almost as far south as the Texas border, destroyed the countryside, burning farms and wiping out what little livestock that remained. Phillips or some of his men would disguise themselves, pretending to be Confederates, would go to the homes at night, tell that they had some wounded comrades, and ask for help. They killed them when the men went to help bring the wounded in. He rode almost as far south as the Texas border, burning homes, barns, and gunning down any that opposed him, in his path to Middle Boggy River.

Middle Boggy

About 20 miles from Fort Washita, the Southerners had a supply depot located along Boggy Depot near present day Atoka. Phillips sent a detachment of 350 men and a section of howitzers under Maj. Charles Willets to seize the outpost.

On February 9, Maj. Willets attacked the Confederate outpost, which had only about 90 men and no cannon. There was a savage battle for about half an hour. The escaping survivors made their way south to the camp of Lt. Col. John Jumper's Seminoles, who rode immediately to Boggy Depot. By the time he arrived, the Union had already pulled out, leaving destruction in their wake. Following their commander's orders of no prisoners, they butchered the wounded Confederates, like hogs with their throats slit open. There were 49 dead. It is still unknown which unit these men belonged to, so therefore, their names are unknown. Fear of the arrival of more Confederate troops influenced the Federals to retire to Fort Gibson.

Col. Phillips' march lasted a month, covering 400 miles, reporting he killed 250 Confederates and returning to Fort Gibson without a single loss. His report did not say that many he killed were innocent civilians. Yet, his mission failed to break the spirit of the Confederacy. The death and destruction he left in his path only served to strengthen the resolve of the Southerners to fight back another year.

The winter was difficult in the Territory, even before Phillip's march. Food was scarce, for the troops and the civilians. The stock was in poor condition, and supplies, such as they were, had to be brought in from Texas. The lack of rains had made the corn and grain crops poor. The troops were poorly clothed, some with no shoes. The Choctaws had no axes with which to get food, firewood or to build shelter. Seminole and Creek troops, with no arms and poor horses did their best to drive out beef for use by the army. Blankets were almost non-existent.

In the spring of 1864, the Confederate forces underwent a change in unit and command structure as Maxey attempted to re-organize his army with the Creek and Seminole Nations' troops brigaded with

Watie's Cherokee troops. This force was designated the 1st Indian Cavalry Brigade and consisted of 1st Cherokee Regiment under Col. Robert C. Parks, 2nd Cherokee Regiment under Col. William Penn Adair (a private that was elected to Col.), Cherokee Battalion under Maj. Joseph A. Scales, 1st Creek Regiment under Col. Daniel N. McIntosh, 2nd Creek Regiment under Col. Chilly McIntosh, the Creek Squadron under Capt. R. Kennard, the Osage Battalion under Major Broke Arm (these warriors were the minority of the Osage Tribe who cast their lot with the Confederacy), the Seminole Battalion under Lt. Col. John Jumper. The commander of the First Indian Cavalry Brigade was Col. Stand Watie.

The Second Indian Cavalry Brigade was composed of the remainder of all Confederate Indian Military Units. They were the First Chickasaw Battalion under Lt. Col. Lemuel M. Reynolds, First Choctaw Battalion under Lt. Col. Jackson McCurtain, First Choctaw and Chickasaw Regiment under Lt. Col. James Riley, Second Choctaw Regiment under Col. Simpson Folsom, and the Reserve Squadron consisting of warriors of the Caddo Tribe under Capt. George Washington, who was the Caddo chief. The commander of the Second Indian Cavalry Brigade was the Confederate hero of the Battle of Newtonia, MO, Col. Tandy Walker. Walker was a mixed blood Choctaw and had been the Choctaw's first principle chief after the tribe's settlement west of the Mississippi.

Col. Walker's first duty after becoming commander of the 2nd Indian Cavalry Brigade was to accompany Gen. Maxey and Col. Richard Gano's Texas Brigade to Arkansas to help Gen Price's army hold back a Federal army under Gen. Fredrick Steele coming out from Union held Little Rock. Soon, Col. Walker found himself in the middle of one of the most infamous battles in the Civil War at Poison Springs, Arkansas (located south and east of Arkadelphia) on April 18, 1864.

This became the end of the Red River Campaign, the last Federal invasion of Confederate Territory in Arkansas. Its aim was to capture Shreveport Louisiana, open Texas for Federal occupation, and acquire the much-needed cotton for Yankee Textile mills in New England. The campaign failed as the result of several battles and skirmishes in Arkansas and Louisiana.

In Louisiana, the battles were at Mannsfield, April 8, Pleasant Hill on April 9 and Monet's Ferry on April 7. In Arkansas, Prairie D'Ann April 10 and Poison Springs, April 18th.Marks Mills April 25, Jenkins Ferry April 30.

Poison Springs, Arkansas

On March 23, 1864, Federal Major General Fredrick Steele, who had captured Little Rock the previous September, left Arkansas's capitol with an army of 13,000 men, 9, 000 horses and mules, 800 wagons, and 30 pieces of artillery. He was under orders to join Major Banks who was leading an amphibious army up the river from New Orleans. In the plan of operations, there were to be three columns converging upon Shreveport within the Southern lines, each column starting from such distant points as New Orleans, Vicksburg, Little Rock, and Fort Smith. When the Federal columns were in motion and well advanced in the direction of the common point of concentration, General E. Kirby Smith, commanding the Trans-Mississippi Department was able to concentrate Confederate forces and attack either Federal column he felt he was strong enough to defeat.

He met the main columns under General Banks at Mansfield, and after a fierce battle with the Federals at a disadvantage, defeated him, and drove back his army to Alexandria, with heavy losses of men, guns, and material. The navy gunboats narrowly escaped trapped above the Falls or Rapids at Alexandria, with a rapidly falling river.

The Confederates frequently harassed Steel, meeting heavy resistance at the crossings of the Little Missouri River and Prairie D'Ann near Prescott. Because resistance was intensifying, Steele abandoned plains to go directly to Shreveport. He turned east and reached Camden Ark. on April 15.

More than 3 weeks of marching and fighting had depleted Steele's supplies. His troops had been on half rations for more than 2 weeks, and unauthorized foraging was wide spread. The capture of a boatload of corn on the Washita River below Camden provided some relief, but on April 17, Steele sent out a massive foraging party, 180 wagons guarded by 870 infantrymen, under the command of Col James M. Williams. They were to collect all the corn and foodstuffs in the area west of Camden.

Federal foragers ranged north and south of the Upper Washington Road taking clothing, jewelry silverware, pots, pans and household items, as well as food and forage. So thorough were the Yankee foragers that their 198 wagons filled to overflowing. As word spread of the heartless foraging raid, cries for revenge swept Confederate camps throughout southwest AR.

On the night of April 17, Confederate scouts found the wagon train camped on White Oak Creek, 16 miles west of Camden. Federal couriers informed Gen. Steele of the train's location and he immediately dispatched reinforcements. These troops commanded by Captain William M. Duncan raised the wagon trains escort to 2500 infantry, including the First Kansas Colored Volunteers Regiment, 90 cavalrymen and a 4-gun battery of Artillery. Early reports of the Federal forage party reported 20 wagons escorted by 200 cavalry dispatched on the 17th.

Based on this information the Third Missouri Cavalry moved to attack the rear of the column. A later report identified 200 wagons, a regiment of cavalry, 2 black infantry regiments, and 3 pieces of artillery. The cavalry was quickly recalled. General Marmeduke wrote General Price recommending a strong concentration of troops to cut the Federals off from Camden.

Sunrise on the 18th, Marmaduke marched his men to the Upper Washington Road. While placing them across the road at Poison Springs, the reinforcements sent by Price arrived, Maxey's Division, then Wood's 14 Missouri Battalion. Marmaduke's plan called for Maxey's division to attack the Federals, the balance of the Confederates would block the road to Camden. About 9:30 am, Federal scouts made contact with the Confederates at Poison Springs. Col Williams parked his wagons 3 abreast, as close together as possible. He ordered the First Kansas to the front forming a line and the cavalry on his flanks. He immediately sent word to Captain Duncan to disperse his troops to protect the rear. Simultaneously Col Williams saw Maxey's Indians and Texans moving on his right flank and sent orders for Duncan to send help to the front. The courier returned with the news that the foe was advancing against Duncan and he could spare no men. The Confederates opened a devastating fire of artillery, advanced in front, and flank. The left of Marmaduke's line advanced double quick through fields and thickets, opening fire as they neared the Federal line.

Under pressure along his entire line, Williams ordered Duncan to re-deploy and cover the retreat of the First Kansas. Williams attempted to make a stand several times, but was overwhelmed each time. This forced the Union troops into the woods north of the road. Outnumbered, Williams defended the train as long as possible, hoping for reinforcements from Camden. After a short and hotly contested engagement at close range, the black troops broke ranks and retreated in chaos. The Confederates cut them down right and left, with a ravaging fire as they tried to escape.

The Federals finally broke to the north in a complete rout, abandoning their artillery, wagons, and spoils, in an effort to escape the howling Indians and westerners. The Confederates pursued the Federals for more than 2 miles before Gen. Maxey, fearing Federal reinforcements, stopped the pursuit, to concentrate on securing the wagon train.

According to Confederate Col. Charles DeMorse, the wagons were laden with corn, bacon, stolen bed quilts, women's and children's clothing, hogs, geese and all the etcetera of unscrupulous other plunder. Shortly after the battle, owners reclaimed their possessions, at Woodlawn the headquarters of Gen. Price. When the shattered survivors of the battle straggled back to Camden, feelings ran high among Steele's troops that the train had been sent out with such a small escort. Its capture aggravated the critical supply situation. Meat was still in supply but the hardtack was completely exhausted. Things looked brighter on the 20th when a supply train arrived from Pine Bluff with 10 days half rations. However, this proved to be the prelude to Marks Mills.

In this battle Union troops numbered 1134, with 236 killed and 65 wounded, 125 captured. C.S.A. troops numbered 3335, 16 killed, 88 wounded, 10 missing. They captured 170 wagons with 6 mule teams, 2 James rifles with caissons, hundreds of small arms, 2 mountain howitzers, with caissons.

Due to their reputation for fierce fighting, Col Williams positioned the First Kansas colored infantry to guard the train against the heaviest Confederate onslaught. They successfully repulsed two enemy attacks, with heavy losses. Denied reinforcements, they gave way on the 3rd. attack. The First Kansas suffered a high proportion of dead to wounded, 117 killed, 65 wounded, largely because the Confederates took no black prisoners.

Steele lost 2750 casualties, lost 635 wagons, 2500 mules, a large number of sutler and refugee wagons, The Confederates had 2500 casualties and lost 35 wagons with no strategic advantage gained by either side.

Black soldiers in the war west of the Mississippi were well aware of their extraordinary position of danger on the battlefield. They knew if they were over run in battle by the Confederates, they would most likely be killed instead of taken prisoner. Moreover, if they were lucky enough to become prisoners, they would be returned to slavery. Back in June 1863, General Edmund Kirby Smith, commander of the Confederate Trans-Mississippi Department had issued orders that all black troops and their white officers given no quarter in battle, no prisoners taken. Although there was a similar unofficial rule in the war in the east, out west it was an unquestioned, documented, official order.

The physiology behind the Confederate soldiers' total lack of mercy for black prisoners is explained in several ways. Perhaps the Southerners sought vengeance on former servants they felt had dared rise up against their masters, which cost thousands of lives. A lot of Southerners were deeply religious and many believed the bible condoned slavery, such as Titus, Chapter 2, "Exhort servants to be obedient unto their own masters, and to please them well in all things: not purloining, but showing good fidelity; that they may adorn the doctrine of God or Savior in all things." Ironically, many Confederates did not own slaves they could not afford them.

After his return from Poison Springs, Maxey stepped up Rebel military action in the Territory, sending out more cavalry patrols. All this activity by the Confederates south of the Arkansas, discouraged all attempts at farming by the Union refugees that had returned from Kansas and the new influx of Indian families arriving at Fort Gibson seeking food and protection swelled greatly the number of refugees already camped there to around 16,000. In the midst of all this, word arrived that a steamboat carrying supplies from Fort Smith up the Arkansas had been attacked and captured.

The Union refugees in Kansas were homesick. On May 16, 1864, the Indian refugee train moved out of the Sauk and Fox Reservation headed for Indian Territory. Over 5,000 Union Indians headed home. About 3,000 men women and children walked with, ahead and behind the wagons, which stretched for six miles. About 2,000 elderly, mothers, and babies rode the wagons with their bedding, pens of chickens and ducks with about 3,500 puppies and dogs as escorts. Behind the refugee wagons, was a train of over 300 wagonloads of supplies headed for the sutlers, McDonald and Fuller at Fort Gibson. All eyes were on the horizons, as rumors were that Watie and Quantrill were waiting for them just below the horizon.

Thirty-one days later, the refugees made it into Fort Gibson, the only problem on the trip, when a band of marauding Osage stole 30 oxen one night. Somehow, they had gotten by Stand Watie's demon Cherokee. What they did not know was - there was no longer a Colonel Stand Watie.

On May 10, Jefferson Davis had signed a commission for a new Brigadier General. Elias C. Boudinot was extremely proud, for the new Brigadier General was Stand Watie! If ever this rank was earned, it was by this fighting little Cherokee, whose name was known, not only in the Territory, but also in the very homeland of his Yankee foes. When the news reached the Territory, his men of the first and second Cherokee, marched around his tent with yells, whoops, fife and beating drums! To hell with John Ross, living well in Philadelphia, and hovering around Lincoln, or his blasted Pin Indians! How could the Rebel Cherokee lose when they fought on the right side, with the South, under a gallant and ferocious soldier and gentleman, whose motivation was his love of this Nation!

Pleasant Bluff, IT

The battle of Poison Spring had shown General Maxey what desperate resistance a small detachment of Federal troops could make when attacked by vastly superior numbers, charged with guarding a supply train, which separated the different units and prevented them from fighting as a single unit. He had seen how these troops, when the Confederates had formed directly across their retreat, had cut their way through with well directed volleys of their rifles, to continue their march.

From about the middle of April to 10 May, Colonel W. P. Adair, with 325 mounted men of the First and Second Cherokee Regiments of Colonel Watie's Brigade, managed to cross the Arkansas below Fort Gibson, and made a raid up through the Cherokee Nation as far as Maysville and Cowskin Prairie. They caused a good deal of excitement among the loyal Indians and the people of southern Kansas, southwest Missouri, and northwest Arkansas, because definite information was not being found as to what point, if any, he would attack.

Federal scouts sent out to try to locate Adair's troops, but when they got to where he was supposedly camped, he was gone. He had crossed the Grand River to the west side, rapidly moving south, crossed the Arkansas above Fort Gibson, to report to Colonel Watie. Most of his troops had deserted in the Cherokee Nation. These deserters gave the loyal Indians a good deal of trouble, some ended as fatal clashes. This information reported to Fort Gibson and mounted detachments sent out to quiet the areas.

Union forces were hard pressed that summer of 1864 to protect their wagon trains and hay stations. All supplies had to be hauled in, because the war had destroyed the Territory north of the Arkansas. Two Federal invasions, foraging by the Confederates and thefts by swarms of bushwhackers left little for survival. Once plentiful, the horses and cattle were gone. The area around Cabin Creek, stripped bare, the buildings of the village gone, was typical of the region. Despite all this, the Federals sent more than 5,000 refugees from Kansas into Indian Territory in June. These would also need to be fed.

Confederate forces were also in bad shape. The Southerners were often dressed in rags, almost shoeless, wearing parts of old uniforms and armed with a variety of old weapons. Still, they kept the Union soldiers from wondering too far from their fortifications. Raiding Confederate Regulars and bands of armed Southern sympathizers threatened Federal communications, shot up hay camps, and tied down thousands of Federal troops.

June brought a rise in the Arkansas, so supplies for Fort Gibson could be sent by boat. The Federals knew that General Cooper's forces had been operating south of the Arkansas, in the areas of North Fork and the upper Poteau valley, within forty to fifty miles of the Federal position at Fort Smith. There were no Federal outposts between Fort Gibson and Fort Smith along the Arkansas. The country was open and the river easily accessed at almost any place for forty to fifty miles. Since General Maxey had the advantage, with any safety, Federal outposts could not be kept out more than ten to fifteen miles. They would have been in constant danger of attack. Scouts from Fort Gibson could not patrol south of the Arkansas, because the Arkansas, above and blow the fort was past fording, making it not safe to be caught on the south side.

The steam ferryboat the *J. R. Williams*, kept at Fort Smith for ferrying men and supplies to Fort Gibson was loaded with a cargo of commissary goods, quartermaster supplies and some sutler goods for the troops at Fort Gibson. Lieutenant G. W. Houston, quartermaster of the Fourteenth Kansas Cavalry and captain of the boat was ordered to take the supplies up river. There was an escort of twenty-six men of the Fourteenth under Lieutenant H. A. B. Cook was sent, but no cavalry escort sent along the south side of the river to guard against the boat being fired upon.

Stand Watie's First Indian Cavalry Brigade were sent to the Arkansas. They moved along the Butterfield Overland Mail route to Pleasant Bluff on the south bank of the Arkansas River and waited. At this point, which was about five miles below the mouth of the Canadian, the Arkansas was about 350 yards wide, and a boat could not pass without coming close to the south side. Their orders were to watch for loaded crafts heading from Fort Smith to Federal forces at Fort Gibson. They set up three artillery pieces overlooking the river hidden behind clusters of brush; about one hundred yards apart on the bluff, and concealed a detachment of Indians in the brush.

As the *"Williams"* came into range, a young officer, Creek Lt. George Washington Grayson, who had returned from school to enlist as a private at age 18, shouted the command to fire! The Confederate guns opened up with thunderous accuracy, hitting the smoke stack, pilothouse, and then the boiler spewed steam all over the deck. At the same time, the Southern Indians opened fire from their concealed positions on shore, hidden from the view of the men on the boat. Taken completely by surprise, they knew nothing of the presence of the Confederate troops until they heard to roar of cannons and muskets.

The 25-man escort, under Lt. Horace Cook, of the 12th Kansas Infantry, returned fire with their rifles as the steamer ran aground on the north bank across from Watie's men. Cook hoped to be able to defend the boat, with the river between them. He soon saw the ship's captain and another officer rowing a yawl toward the south shore. Now the Confederates had a way to reach him! Cook and his men jumped overboard and fled into the brush across the river. The Captain, pilot, a white woman, and a Negro woman were taken prisoner. Two of the men separated and made their way about ten miles to Mackey's Salt Works in the Cherokee Nation where Colonel John Ritchie was stationed with the Second Indian Regiment. He immediately took two hundred of his men and headed for the site.

Watie's men secured the ship and attached ropes managing to maneuver it closer to a sand bar on the south side. The cargo consisted of hominy, dried and smoked pork and other groceries and extensive assortment of dry goods for the sutlers at the fort. About 150 barrels were taken and Watie's Confederates had new clothes - Yankee uniforms!

Watie sent word back for wagons to carry the goods. The food was in great need by the soldiers and the refugees. While waiting for wagons to come from General Cooper, word came that the Federals were coming from Fort Smith, so Watie ordered the men to carry what they could and burn the rest. A 200-man detachment of the Union Second Indian Home Guard rode out from their camp 10 miles away and arrived on the scene, opening fire on Watie's remaining troops. Before withdrawing, Watie set the steamboat afire; quickly engulfing the wooden vessel, which slipped beneath the river. How Watie would have loved being at Fort Gibson when the news came to his old foe, Colonel Phillips! Also taken in the raid were papers and letters, one from the chief quartermaster's office in Fort Smith to Lt. Huston 14th Kansas, regarding the shipment, and the same to Colonel Phillips, Commanding at Fort Gibson.

The Federal supply line on the Arkansas was broken. In addition, the hungry Union Indians at Fort Gibson learned that Stand Watie had not forgotten to give them a bite, not of the supplies, but of his cunning and power. The hungry Indians became even sicker when they heard the news that the supplies that Watie could not haul away, were floating down the river. It was certain that the Pins that stayed under the Union flag would do so....hungry!

Confederate outposts were moving closer to Fort Smith as Watie's troops continued destroying road-hauled goods. On June 27, 1864, the military Cherokee units gathered at Watie's camp at Limestone Prairie. There the Cherokee troops unanimously re-enlisted in the Army of the Confederacy for the duration of the war. With the ongoing struggle in Indian Territory, the Cherokee were exiles from their home country. Because of the treachery of their leaders, Cherokee Country was in the hands of the Union. Riding with Watie had made the names of the Cherokee Regiment household words in both North and South. Regardless of the weather, the Cherokee continually harassed the enemy. Nevertheless, Cherokee country, north of the Arkansas was in Union hands, the wives and children of the soldiers having to flee south into Choctaw Country. Refugees from the Creek and northern Choctaw counties, pushed farther, gathered along the Red River and in Texas.

During the previous winter, Stand Watie's nephew, Cherokee Representative Elias C. Boudinot, had been busy in the Congress of the Confederacy, lobbying for and getting a loan or appropriation for $100,000 to purchase food and supplies for the troops and civilians. A general council meeting on July 20, at Choteau's Trading House, discussed legislative action for the welfare of the Nation. Cherokee representatives were Tusy Guess, John Chambers, and William Arnold.

Although nothing significant was gained by Watie's steamboat adventure, his sensational exploit electrified Southern sympathizers in the region, boasting their morale and inspiring them to carry on the war effort. Soon after his victory at Pleasant Bluffs, near present day Tahama, OK Stand Watie received orders notifying him of his promotion to Brigadier General, retro active to May 10, 1864. Watie became the only American Indian to obtain the rank of General in the war.

General Watie's fame as the greatest Confederate Indian continued to spread. His Cherokee Regiment raided along the Fort Smith-Fort Gibson Road, pounding hooves, shrill Cherokee Rebel yell, and blazing guns. They were like dust in the wind, ever on the move, doing their damage and scampering out of reach. Riding with them, cheering them on, were the spirits of the fallen comrades as shadows in the dust. Their torches claimed Union haystacks, mowing equipment, as their bullets claimed Union Indians and African soldiers.

Massard Prairie, Arkansas

The continuance fighting between Maxey and Cooper, which took up more time than fighting the Yankees, finally ended on July 21st, when a directive arrived from the Confederate secretary of State making Indian Territory a separate Military district and putting General Cooper in charge. At last, Cooper was in total charge of the Territory and the most impoverished, undisciplined and demoralized troops in the whole Confederacy. He had been handed a rusty broken sword to fight a hopeless battle against overwhelming odds. He saddled up for a bold march into Arkansas, briefly diverting Union attention to Fort Smith.

On July 27, a detachment of Choctaws and Texans led by Colonel Richard Gano and Watie's Cherokee sprang a devastating surprise attack on a Union cavalry outpost on Massard Prairie south of Fort Smith. Several companies of the Sixth Kansas Cavalry under Major David Mefford manned it. He rallied his men in a desperate fighting retreat toward the Union camp at Fort Smith. Before they reached Fort Smith, their horses stampeded, and overwhelming numbers of hard riding Rebel Warriors surrounded the dismounted troopers.

General Gano concentrated his force during the night on the Poteau River about ten miles southwest of the Federal camp and moving forward before daybreak drove in the pickets before sunrise, his advance arriving at major Mefford's camp, almost with the pickets. The firing between the advance and the pickets had alerted the camp and Mefford got his men out in line before Gano's charge. He ordered his herd brought in from the prairie where it was grazing. Before the herd could be secured and the men mounted, Gano charged the camp and stampeded the horses, leaving Major Mefford with his command dismounted to make the best fight possible with the overwhelming force of Texans and Indians.

Unfortunately, Mefford's camp was in the edge of the timber on the south side of Massard Prairie and there was no shelter to protect the Federals. He was able to fight off three charges, before the Confederates had passed around his flanks and formed at his rear, forcing a retreat across the prairie in the direction of Fort Smith.

After fighting a retreat for over a mile, Medford, not being able to break through the Confederate line, surrendered, 127 Yankees captured including Major Mefford and Lieutenant J. M. Friese., 11 killed and 20 wounded. Gano's losses were nine dead and 26 wounded. Reinforcements were on their way from Fort Smith, so Watie turned his command back toward safety. The dismounted captives had to double time it for 10 miles. It was a very warm day and the prisoners were nearly exhausted and suffered from thirst. After crossing the Poteau River, they stopped for the night. With a sufficient escort, the prisoners were taken to Tyler Texas, where the Confederate stockade and prison was, to keep the prisoners captured west of the Mississippi.

Fort Smith, Arkansas

Major Howland took about 300 raiders from the Cherokee and Creek Regiments north of the Verdigris and attacked a haying crew, burning the hay. On July 30, General Cooper advanced on the strong Union force at Fort Smith with his small-scale, ragged army. General Watie, who was now commander of both Indian Brigades with Cooper's promotion, helped drive back the Union troops before the Fort's defenses.

General Watie sent the First Cherokee Regiment under Colonel Bell on the main road and Colonel Adair on to the left along the road called Line Road. Both units charged with their usual vigor, chasing them into Fort Smith. They pulled back to the Federal camp that had just been the scene of a fast eviction, and where the Federals had left a tasty meal.

General Gano, having been promoted, arrived with Captain Humphreys light battery, and advanced to open fire on the Federals about 700 yards in front. The Federals brought up a four-gun battery and opened fire, the shells falling on the light artillery. One shell landed among the horses and the resulting explosion killed three horses, wounded one, and beheaded one man, severed the leg of another. The Confederates pulled back again into the Territory.

The Confederate guerilla warfare continued during the late summer, with small but deadly Rebel cavalry raids. In August, Stand Watie with about 500 men pulled off a raid at Gunter's Prairie north of the Arkansas. Watie seized prisoners, horses, and mules burned hay and caused further panic among his enemies. This was at a time when the Southern Cause in the region seemed doomed beyond recovery; the Confederates scored their largest victory in the Territory since 1861.

Also in August, intelligence reached Watie that another large supply train was loading to move south the Military Road from Fort Scott to Fort Gibson. A few days later Watie talked to Brigadier General Samuel B. Maxey, his superior, proposing a major raid on Union communications and supplies in the area. He asked General Gano to join him on this raid, to bypass Fort Gibson and capture or destroy this "million dollar" Yankee treasure. They agreed the prize was worth the risk. Because Gano had been promoted to Brigadier General one month before Watie, they agreed he would be officially in charge. Both men agreed that each would maintain command of their own men, though they would act together.

Flat Rock, IT

With this train in mind, a strong force of Confederate cavalry was ordered up the Grand River valley above Fort Gibson. On September 16, 1864, eight hundred men of the 1st Indian Cavalry Brigade of Cherokee, Choctaw, Chickasaws, John Jumper's Creeks and Seminoles, under General Stand Watie and 1,200 men of the newly promoted General Richard Gano's Texas Brigade, 29th, 30th, and 31st Cavalry and Captain Sylvanus Howell's battery of 6 guns, moved out. Moving around Union positions as they rode north, the Indians and Texans thundered into the Grand River Valley about 15 miles above Fort Gibson, with about 2,000 troops and 6 artillery pieces. Knowing the Confederate column could be detected at any time, Gano sent Major John Vann ahead with a Cherokee Regiment to scout the area below the Arkansas and check as far north as possible.

The Gano-Watie column crossed the Arkansas River near the Creek Agency. Since the river was high, it took six hours for the column to cross. Men on foot carried the munitions boxes over their heads and the horses crossed with the cannon munitions. That evening they camped just eleven miles northwest of Fort Gibson at Camp Pleasant, four miles south of Chosky in the Creek Nation.

At Flat Rock Creek, two miles from the Grand River, a large Federal hay camp was in operation, scattered over 3 miles of prairie - cutting and putting up hay. The Union officer, Captain E. A. Barker had 125 men including a small unit of the Second Kansas Calvary and a detachment of the First Kansas Colored Infantry. Because of the guerilla activity, Captain

Barker kept small cavalry patrols on 24 hours a day scouting the country around his camp. Flat Rock Creek, a tributary of the Grand River, was an oasis on the prairie. There were numerous pools connected by ribbons of water along the clear little stream. The pools lined with small willows and brush, presented a cool retreat for the soldiers working all day in the hot late summer sun.

Late afternoon, one of the cavalry patrols came galloping back into camp. They had seen "hundreds and hundreds" of Rebel soldiers coming their way along the old military road. Barker ordered his men in from the hay fields; nervously they grabbed their weapons and ran to a ravine along the back of the camp. Meanwhile, Generals Watie and Gano stood on a high hill, watching the operation through their field glasses. What a coup this would be! They would be playing in the enemies' back yard - and special playmates would be the Corps D'Afrique, as the Confederates called the Negro troops.

Barker and his escort rode out to see the enemy. He hoped they had been mistaken, that it was only a detachment passing. As they topped a ridge on the prairie, he was horrified to see 2,000 Rebels coming toward him. Barker and his escort wheeled their horses and rode back to the camp followed close behind by the enemy. By the time they had reached the ravine, the Texans and Indians were about 200 yards behind and started a fierce attack from five points. The little Union force, outnumbered about 20 to one, fought off three Confederate Calvary charges in the next hour.

Knowing they would soon be over run, Barker mounted what men that could find their horses, and made a desperate charge against the Confederate line. With pistols blazing, Barker and 40 troopers charged straight into the line of Watie's Warriors. The captain and about 15 of his troopers made it through the enemy line and ran for the fort. They left the dismounted cavalrymen and the colored troops to fight their way to the Grand River----if they could.

Barker later reported:

"After fighting them for half an hour, and finding myself completely overwhelmed and surrounded, and my position every moment becoming more and more intenable, I determined to charge them with my mounted men, and order the infantry and dismounted cavalry to make the rest of their way to the Grand River timber, about a mile distant. Mounting my men and selecting the weakest point in their lines, I made at them with a rush they could not withstand and succeeded in cutting my way through, with a loss of all but fifteen men. The whole force of the enemy charged into my camp, capturing all the white soldiers remaining there, and killing all the colored soldiers they could find. Only four out of the thirty seven of them succeeded in making their escape. The enemy captured and destroyed all my camp and garrison equipage, company books, and papers of every description pertaining to my company. Also a quantity of ordinance and ordinance stores....for which I was responsible. Also 12 US mules and two 6-mule wagons and harness, which were burned, together with all the mowing machines, wagons, &c., belonging to the hay contractors. My whole loss is 40 killed; wounded; missing, and prisoners, 66."

The First Kansas Colored troops rallied under their lieutenant, Thomas B. Sutherland, for their last stand. They knew their chances of escaping alive were slim, but they were determined their lives would come at a very high coast. Firing their Springfields from their scant shelter, they fought off several attacks for two hours, as their numbers got smaller. With his ammunition gone, Lt. Sutherland gave the order, every man for himself. They split up and ran for their lives as the expected massacre happened. Some of the Negroes ran from the tall weeds and unburned haystacks pleading to be spared, but the Texans and Confederate Indians had not sympathy for the Union Negroes, shooting them down. Some that escaped hid in the shallow pools with just their nose above water. About one in five got away.

General Gano later wrote of the encounter "The setting sun witnessed our complete success as it's last lingering rays rested upon a field of blood. Seventy three Federals, mostly Negroes, lay dead." The Rebels also burned an estimated three to five thousand tons of hay, before moving on north on the Texas Road to find the wagon train. Again, Fort Gibson would suffer Stand Watie's wrath.

Irregular warfare was now the common thing, particularly where the Cherokee Champion, Stand Watie, led. For a man like him, "surrender" was not in his vocabulary, and utter despair was out of the question. He was ready to risk everything, at any moment, on the next roll of the dice. Where he led, his Southern Indians followed, without question.

Second Cabin Creek, IT

From prisoners taken at Flat Rock, General Watie and General Richard Gano, Fifth Texas Calvary Brigade, learned that the large Union supply train they hoped to find, was expected at Fort Gibson from Fort Scott, Kansas. A train of 205 government wagons and 91 sutler wagons with armed teamsters had left the Kansas post September 12, escorted by 260 men of the 2nd, 6th, and 14th Kansas Calvary, commanded by Major Henry Hopkins

The Confederates headed on north to camp near the site of present day Salina, on Wolf Creek. Now that they were in Union held territory, there was more urgency in the troops. Gano and Watie extended their scouting of the Military Road to the east branch, just in case the train had taken that route. They did not want the train to slip through their grasp. They spotted a hay camp on Hickory Farm, but decided not to attack, as the sound would alert the train.

On September 18, Gano, with about 400 Texans scouted north to locate the train, Watie waited in camp, so the main force would not be seen. About 3:00 in the afternoon, Gano spotted the train parked at Cabin Creek. The white canvas tops left no doubt then train had been found. They were parked across the landscape, behind the stockade, in the timber along the creek and on the bluff. Many were loosely parked; their teams unhitched, and horses grazing, for about a mile on the prairie south of the creek. Then, hiding in the trees, Gano sent word back for Watie to join him. The train had been located! However, Union spies had sighted the Confederates. Word quickly spread that Watie was on the prowl and a message was sent to the train to "run for safety to any place with a stockade!"

While camped at Horse Creek on September 17, the Major received a dispatch from Fort Gibson, telling him of a large Confederate advance to the north. It ordered him to take his supply train to the Union post at Cabin Creek where 170 Cherokee troops of the 2nd Indian Home Guard and 140 troops of the 3rd Indian Home Guard staffed the post. This gave Major Hopkins over 600 men to guard his wagons. Following the Texas road, the train reached the crossing at Cabin Creek on September 18, 1864, where 310 Union Cherokees of the Second and Third Home Guards met it.

He pulled the train to a stop on a bluff overlooking the crossing. His men and the teamsters quickly stacked hay bales around the wagons to reinforce the stockade. Major Hopkins was under the impression that Yankee troops and guns were moving from Fort Gibson and Fort Smith to help protect the train. Without reinforcements, Hopkins had about 1,000 white and Indian troops to protect over 400 wagons and 1,800 mules and horses.

There were 205 government owned wagons and teams, loaded with commissary and quartermaster supplies as well as four ambulances and ninety sutlers' wagons. The quartermaster wagons carried clothing, blankets, and shoes intended for the refugees at Fort Gibson.

Only hours after the 300 plus wagons arrived at Cabin Creek, Col. Gano's Confederate scouts found them. From what the Major's scouts had told him, he thought the Confederate force could not be more than 800 men and no artillery.

By midnight, Watie had arrived with the rest of the Confederate troops and the artillery. He and Colonel Gano decided to advance on the Union position by moonlight and when they were about a half mile from the Union position, deployed for battle, Watie's force on the left, Gano's on the right and the six gun artillery in the center. They could hear the men inside the stockade drinking and shouting. Silent as the moonlight, they moved toward the enemy.

As they advanced to within 300 yards of the Federal position, a volley of Union gunfire blazed through the air. The 2,000 Southerners then opened up with their shoulder weapons, showing the full strength of their force. Hopkins strained his eyes in the dark to see their long double lines of troops.

Then, to his utter horror, six cannon suddenly roared to life from the center of the Rebel lines. The artillery rounds tore through tents, timber, and wagons, exploding in blinding flashes all around the stockade. The noise panicked the supply train mules. The terrified animals broke into a blind stampede plunging over the high banks into the creek, taking the wagons with them. Many of the teamsters cut mules loose from tangled harnesses, mounted them, and headed north to Fort Scott. The hell of gunfire continued through the night and a number of Union soldiers chose to withdraw early and faded into the night. Some claim that Major Hopkins also joined the early retreat but the charges were never proven.

Along the Confederate line, individual Indians shouted their traditional turkey gobble challenge to the Pins inside. In the melee of exploding Confederate shells, burning wagons, screaming Indians and wounded animals realized he could not depend on relief from the Forts. He decided to try to save what he could of the train and head for Fort Scott. However, it seems, Watie read his mind, as two of his regiments took possession of the road to Fort Scott, cutting off any retreat that direction.

At dawn, the Confederate troops gradually moved to partially encircle the Union forces left, catching the battered Yanks in a deadly crossfire. Federal soldiers lay flat on the ground to escape fire, some of the animals in total panic, ran over the 150-foot bluff. Still Major Hopkins held on, just maybe those six companies of Union Indians would arrive out of the smoke. The Rebels drove in the Union right, forcing it around to the west, then Gano's Texans moved in on the new flank.

Under the cover of the billowing smoke and gunpowder, Hopkins ordered his troops to leave the wagons and fight their way out to Fort Gibson. Finally, the out-numbered, out-gunned Union soldiers withdrew, retreating toward Fort Gibson. The Seminoles drove all the way through to the road. Behind the fleeing Federals, Watie's Cherokee fired the hayricks, which created additional confusion. By 9:00 a.m., the Federals had been driven from the field, leaving their wagon train ---as well as their dead and wounded--- for anyone who might want it. The Confederates were more interested in the wagon train than a few escaping Yankees.

The victorious Rebels burned the disabled wagons along with about 3,000 tons of hay and killed the crippled mules. The Confederates salvaged the stores of 710 mules and 130 wagons, loaded them heavily with clothing, raw foodstuffs, ammunition. Nothing usable was left of the train, except what was in Confederate hands. The captured wagon train transformed the ragged, half starved Confederate force into a well fed, properly equipped and nearly uniformed little army, as it started them "way down south in Dixie". In the battle, only 20 Union and 9 Confederates were killed. The rebels were aware that Federal troops were near and could show up at any minute.

General Gano wrote in his report:

"At 9 o'clock (six hours after the first volley was fired), the field was ours, with more than $1,000,000 worth of Federal property in our hands. We burned all the broken wagons and killed all the crippled mules. We brought off 130 wagons and 740 mules. We clothed 2,000 men of the expedition so as to make them comfortable for the present and have some commissaries on hand."

This action, known as the second Battle of Cabin Creek, not far from the present day Big Cabin, OK, convinced people on both sides that the Confederates in Indian Territory were not a weak, defeated rabble of washed-up warriors, but a rather dangerous force of hardened veterans who were still a threat to the Federal

Government. They had given the Yankees their worst disaster in Indian Territory. The Civilized Nations had scored their most impressive military triumph, which echoed from Richmond to Texas and the Confederate Indians along the Red River and in Texas, renewed hopes for an Indian South.

Pryor Creek, IT

Moving the wagon train south, about 4:30, Watie and Gano ran into a strong Union Infantry at Pryor Creek, making a forced march to assist Major Hopkins at Cabin Creek. The commander was Col. James Williams, who had led the First Kansas Colored Brigade to victory at the first Cabin Creek. Now, he faced the victors of the second Cabin Creek. Williams was outnumbered 2 to 1 and fell back to a defensive position with his First and 2nd Colored Infantry as well as the battery of highly accurate long-range artillery pieces known as Parrott Rifles. The deadly guns drove back the Confederate advance.

Gano and Watie unlimbered their artillery and both sides dueled for an hour. At dusk, Gano deployed most of his troops in a long battle line on a high ridge in full view of Williams and his men, while the wagon train rushed forward behind the lines, heading for the Verdigris River. Camping on the George May farm that night, the Confederates built fires along the ridge to create the appearance they were encamped in force. They ran a wagon back and forth over rocky ground to make the Federals believe they were camping for the night, to resume the fight in the morning. At Dawn, Hopkins saw his foes were long gone. Williams' troops had hard marched 80 miles in less than 2 days and were in no shape to follow, especially when they were outnumbered anyway. Gano and Watie crossed the Verdigris at Clem Roger's place near Claremore

Mound. Here Watie discovered his Cherokee had found whiskey in the sutlers' wagons. Knowing what alcohol could do to the discipline and morale on a march, ordered it dumped into the Verdigris. Turning south to the Arkansas River, they crossed about 15 miles above Fort Gibson and on into Tulsey Town.

The weary Confederates arrived at Camp Bragg on the south side of the Canadian River on September 28. They had ridden over 400 miles in 14 days, killed 97, wounded many, took 111 prisoners and whipped the US Army in a fierce little battle that would prove to be the Federal Government's worst defeat in Indian Territory. They burned 6,000 tons of hay, destroyed all reapers and mowers. For 3 days and nights, the Confederates moved the train to Southern Territory. They slept in the saddle or caught quick naps at watering holes. They cut out trees, cut down banks, rolled wagons and artillery up hills by hand. The Commanders reported they kept cheerful and never slacked for a good cause. In all they destroyed $1,500,000.00 worth of Federal property, taking a third of this amount back to their lines. The Confederate loss was 6 killed, 48 wounded, and 3 mortally.

Their military action also turned out to be the last serious clash between the Union and Confederate forces in the Territory. The two Generals worked in perfect harmony to secure the victory.

A telegram, dated September 20, 1864, from Perry Fuller to Commissioner of Indian Affairs, Dole stated;

"Stand Watie has captured government train at Cabin Creek, three hundred troops and two hundred fifty teamsters. Have troops sent to Gibson at once. All demoralized on the border. Something must be done or the Indians will cause trouble. Our loss, sixty thousand dollars."

As reports of the raids went through the ranks of Federal Officers, the Rebel force grew in size. Major General George Sykes wrote from Fort Scott that there were 3,000 Rebels at Cabin Creek. Colonel C. W. Blair reported the Rebels at 4,000 strong.

Rumors flew as Union officers plotted to capture Watie. Colonel Jennison contemplated an all out effort to repel Watie, as rumors said he was still advancing. One report had Watie and 6,000 Indians 30 miles from Humboldt, and they had burned the Osage Mission. Federal troops were under constant alert, and soldiers needed elsewhere shifted to the Indian Territory border. But Watie and the Rebel Indians were already back in Southern Territory

The battle at Cabin Creek did not alter the course of the war. Loss of the wagon train was only a temporary setback for the Federals. Nevertheless, the victory was a bright spot for Confederate sympathizers, as it came when things were not going well in the east. For the Southern people in Indian Territory, half starved, their land devastated, and their morale at the bottom, it gave them a brief time of happiness. Watie and Gano received a flood of congratulations and the Confederate Congress gave them a vote of thanks.

The autumn of 1864 found things in a bad way in Indian Country. The cold spring, the summer drought, swarms of grasshoppers, chinch bugs, and other insect pests had destroyed the Kansas crops the Federals were depending on to care for the refugees. The Red River campaign of Generals Banks and Steele had ended in disaster. Its failure had dealt a terrific blow to the idea of sending the refugees home. The victory by the Confederates had prevented a general desertion of the Southern Indians to the North. Until that battle, they were about to desert because they were disgusted with their treatment by the South. To obtain this Southern victory, the Confederate Indians staked everything on this last roll of the dice, and received an almost undreamed of success! This lit the fires of Southern sympathy again.

This failure of the Red River Campaign meant the refugees in Kansas would spend another winter on short rations. Farm products were scarce and their regular buffalo hunt had been temporarily forbidden because of the hostilities of the Plains Indians.

In ante-bellum days, Indian Territory had been well stocked. The individual slave holding tribes were rich in cattle, pigs, and ponies. The war took this way of life and turned it upside down. Livestock, crops, and food were requisitioned by the troops.

Throughout the war, a cattle stealing was a regular frontier industry participated in by civilians and soldiers. The criminal activities that decimated the Nations, were condoned, connived, and shared in by agents of the United States. By 1865, it reached scandalous proportions.

Some of the stock driven north into Kansas: some the army used for its needs, but most went to contractors, who sold it to the government at highly inflated prices, for the refugees.

Profiteering on such a tremendous scale and with shameless audacity had never before been known anywhere on the frontier. The Indians were fully aware they were being sold their own cattle at these high prices, but could do nothing.

December 20, 1864, Lewis Downing, acting Principal Chief of the Cherokee sent a memorandum to President Lincoln, outlining a plan devised by the Union Cherokee for defeating the Rebels. This plan, had it been put into effect, could have recalled the Secessionists back to the Union and ended the tribal estrangements and could have prevented many of the things that happened for a decade after the war. A copy of this memo is in the Interior Department files, Office of Indian Affairs, and reads:

"We, the undersigned for ourselves and as the representatives of the Cherokee People, feeling an intense interest in maintaining perpetual harmony and good will among the various tribes of Indians mutually, as well as between these and the people and government of the United States, beg leave, very respectfully, to lay before your Excellency a few facts and suggestions relating to this matter."

"We deem it a matter of vast moment to the Cherokees, Creeks, and Seminoles, and to the State of Kansas and to Nebraska, as well as to the Whole Union, that the perfect friendship of the wild tribes be secured and maintained, while our friendship is of paramount importance to the said tribes: and it is with the deepest regret that we hear of and observe acts of hostility on the part of any Indians, It is our firm conviction that Southern Rebels are, and have bee, instigating the wild tribes to take part in the present rebellion against the Federal government. The depredations recently committed by portions of the some of these tribes on emigrants crossing the western plains, we are forced to regard as the result of such instigations on the part of the rebels."

"There are also indications that these tribes are forming into predatory bands and are engaged in stealing stock in connection with wicked white men who are first loyal and then rebel as best suits their purposes of stealing and robbery."

"As the war progresses and the rebel armies are broken into fragments, the rebels will doubtless scatter among these tribes and will make every effort to organize them into banditti -. Then, when the strength of the rebellion is broken and peace is formally declared and we are off our guard, they will fall upon defenseless neighborhoods of loyal Indians, or whites, and plunder and kill unrestrained."

"The highways to the Pacific States and to the gold regions of the west, they will infest, to harass immigrants and merchants and endanger their property and lives. To keep down such depredations by force of arms will require many men and a vast expense."

"In our opinion no pains should be spared to gain friendship of these people by peaceful means and thus secure their help against the rebels and in favor of the public peace."

"In the year 18?, a general convention of the Indian Tribes was held at Tahlequah in the Cherokee Nation which convened at the call of the Cherokee National Council. Representatives from the Cherokees, Creeks, Seminoles, Chickasaws, Delaware, Shawnees, Osages, Seneca and twelve other nations attended this convention and participated in its deliberations. It was a harmonious, pleasant and profitable meeting of the Red men of the West. Friendship and good will established and a league was entered into by which the most friendly relations were maintained among the various tribes for many years. Arrangements were made for the punishment of crimes committed by the citizens of any nation on those of any other."

"Many years have passed away since the said convention of tribes. Men who were then young now occupy prominent positions and are the rulers of their respective nations, yet they know but little of the harmonious feeling and the amity established among their fathers."

"The long continuation of the present war, together with the lies and machinations of the rebels, operating on these ignorant tribes, have shaken the confidence of some of them in the government of the United States and, to some extent, made the impression that the Cherokees, Creeks and other nations who are in alliance with the Federal government, are the enemies of these wild tribes and that the enemies of the Government are their friends"

"In view of this state of thins we propose that the nations, who are fighting under the banner of the Union, invite all the tribes of the Southwest and as many others as possible to meet in general convention and re-establish their league of amity and re-assert, in solemn council, their loyalty to the Federal government. Let them there, in the presence of the GREAT SPIRIT, give mutual pledges to maintain peace among themselves and with their white brethren, to abstain from all acts of theft, robbery, murder or violence, and to do all in their power to bring justice to any persons, either Indian or whites, who may be guilty of such acts, or may incite others to commit them under any pretext whatever."

"Let them there league together to crush out the rebellion and put an end to the war throughout the country."

"We propose that the said convention of tribes be held near Claremore's Mound, on the Verdigris River, in the Cherokee Nation and that it convene in the early part of next June."

"We all desire very respectfully to request President Lincoln to send a talk signed with his own hand and sealed with the great seal of the United States to this convention. Let him also send a white pipe, and with tobacco and a white flag and the Book of God containing the talk of the GREAT SPIRIT to men. Let it all be wrapped in the flag of the Union and let him send some suitable person to deliver this talk, and on behalf of the President to smoke the pipe of peace with these nations beneath the waves of these flags."

"We would also ask that the President give to military commanders orders to afford proper protection to such convention and to the delegates both in going to and returning from said convention."

"In view of the fact that the war has so desolated our country that the Cherokees cannot, as in former times, provide for the feeding of such a council, we, very relucktantly, ask that such provision be made by the United States."

(Note: The above referenced council, although the date is illegible, could be the council referred to by George Catlin in his "Letters and Notes on the North American Indians" which took place in about 1834)

Most of 1864 had presented a grim picture of the war's prospects from a southern point of view. The boost in morale as the result of the Confederate victory at Cabin creek sent southern spirits soaring in the Nations. The events in the Territory did not match the grand scale of events in the east, but the southern Indians world revolved around him, and to just keep his family fed and clothed through the weary winters of the war, represented quite an accomplishment to him.

The effects of the raid on the Northern command policy had the Federal District commander of Indian Territory, General John M. Thayer, began to panic. They believed that Cooper was planning a full-scale attack on the northern territory. Rumors flew throughout Indian Territory and the command headquarters at Fort Smith and Fort Scott concerning a planned Confederate invasion. Concern became so great that General Edward S. Canby recommended that all of Indian Territory be abandoned and troops withdrawn.

The power of Watie's name and his reputation as a raider were obvious. With a force of less than one thousand men, never well-armed or clothed, often hungry, he was able to keep the Federal troops in such a state of command indecision in the winter of 1864-1865 that they were seriously considering abandoning the entire region. Perhaps in the entirety of the whole Civil War, never were so few men able to apply such a psychological advantage over a more powerful and better-equipped enemy.

The simple fact was both Watie and Cooper were planning to establish winter camps. Although Watie would have liked to mount an attack, he knew the horses and mules and the men of his Confederate Indians needed a rest after their long, hard successful spring and summer campaigns.

The Indian Brigade under Watie's command was now comprised of the First Cherokee Regiment under Colonel Robert C. Parks; the Second Cherokee Regiment under Colonel William P. Adair; a separate Cherokee Battalion under Major Joseph A. Scales; the First Creek Regiment under Colonel Daniel N. McIntosh; The Second Creek Regiment under Colonel Chilly McIntosh; a detached Creek Squadron under Captain R. Kenard; the First Seminole Battalion under Lt. Colonel John Jumper and the First Osage Battalion under Major Broke Arm.

The First Osage and Major Broke Arm was a surprising result of recruitment a couple years before, when Watie had sent his non-Indian staff officer, Thomas F. Anderson out west. Anderson succeeded in raising Broke Arm's Osage Battalion, a large company of Caddos and Arapahos under Captain George Washington, a Caddo, and a company of Comanche under Captain Esopah. The Caddos, Arapahos, and Comanche although somewhat loosely organized, but loyal to Watie. All performed excellent scouting duties rambling between Kansas and the Texas panhandle.

Chapter Eight

1865

Though his men were better dressed now, because of the new uniforms captured at Cabin Creek, General Watie was deeply concerned about the suffering of the Southern Refugee Indians. He sent his adjutant, Lt. Thomas F. Anderson east of the Mississippi to get whatever medicine he could find. General Maxey arranged to feed the refugees from the army commissary, as much as they could. In the beginning, feeding them was easy, because there were few that needed the help. Nevertheless, with the occupation of Cherokee Country north of the Arkansas and the lack of security of the portions of the Choctaw, Creek and Seminole countries close to the Arkansas, hundreds of families had been driven from their homes. They were now in crowded refugee camps in the southern portions of Choctaw and Chickasaw country, numbering between 15,000 and 16,000.

Finding food for the refugees was a major job. The Confederates explored every avenue to obtain money for supplies. They shipped cotton from Lamar Co. TX to Matamoras, Mexico, as a legitimate business, not a wartime speculation.

On February 14, Brigadier General D. H. Cooper was appointed Superintendent of Indian Affairs in the District of Indian Territory. Brigadier General Stand Watie was appointed Commander of the Division of Indian Troops.

In the Northern reports, repeatedly, Stand Watie's Cherokee riders were the most feared by the Yankees. There were reports that Watie was preparing for a raid along the Neosho Valley. Major General Blunt sent word to Major General Dodge, that the people in this valley were alarmed, there was a lot of stock, and the route Watie would come was well supplied with good grass and water.

The start of 1865, a strange twist of fate occurred. With Watie's troops fighting a desperate holding action, their horses worn out, and the men riding day and night on raids, the Plains Indians suddenly wanted to join the Confederate gray. They had signed alliances with Pike back in 1861, and had not helped the Confederate cause any.

Possibly one reason for this change of attitude was caused by Colonel J. M. Chivington's raid on the Cheyenne and Arapaho, in their winter camp on Sand Creek. On November 29, 1864, Chivington and his 900 volunteers out of Denver had attacked Black Kettle's camp, even though he ran up a white flag and a US flag, and massacred hundreds of men, women, and children. If this was the North's "marching to make men free" then these plains survivors wanted none of it.

The first note of this new support came in January when word was received at the headquarters of the Osage Battalion at Camp Dorn that the Comanche and Kiowa wanted to take the warpath against the Federals in the spring. The Osage, in good spirits, were hoping to give 'em hell in Kansas in the summer.

About the first of 1865, an Indian meeting was held at Cherokee town, where the Prairie Indians, the Kiowa, Comanche, and Arapaho visited Tuckabatche Micco, Principle Chief of the Creek. They were anxious to meet with the chiefs of the Confederate Indians. The plains Indians told of several councils where the Yankees tried to get them to take the warpath against the south. The Second Chief of the Comanche, O-hop-ey-a-ne told of the large amount of goods and presents, as well as guns and ammunition that they could have if they would make war on the south. The Yankee officers told them to kill all men and boys and take the women and children prisoner. Next, they were to drive off all cattle and horses. However, when they returned home, they must give up the white women and girls, the Indian women could remain theirs. The mules, horses and cattle, the Yankees would buy.

When the Union officer stopped speaking, the Comanche chief told him he had friends and brothers in the South and he would not make war on them. The Yankee said if he did not fight, he would not get the guns. The Comanche told him he would still kill the buffalo with his bow and arrows and live on the prairie.

Jesse Chisholm, the Cherokee Indian trader, who could speak 14 languages, was the interpreter for this council, and had advised the Indians to not listen to the Northern Man's bad talk.

When Watie received word of this council, he sent Major Vore to the meeting, but the plains Indians had already left.

Many dreaded the coming of spring, 1865, bringing a new series of deadly military campaigns and terrifying guerilla raids. Yet, it was not the same as the previous four had been. Instead, there were only a few scattered shots and most of these did not even hit their targets. Not even the legendary Stand Watie took the field in one of his daring raids. Both sides were sick of death and destruction and avoided each other, waiting the inevitable end that came with Lee's surrender at Appomattox, Virginia, April 9, 1865. Interestingly, there was an Indian officer present at this meeting. Col. Ely Parker, a full blood Seneca, serving on General Grant's staff was one of the few Union Officers present in the McLean home when the papers were signed.

On April 12, General Dodge advised Blunt that he had reliable information that Stand Watie had now a combination of all Southern Indians, except for those known as "pins" for an operation against Kansas. For the next few days, the Federal forces searched for the large contingent of Rebels that was coming to Kansas, but never found him!

In late April 1865, Watie and Cooper were carrying on with their raids against the North, to "Give Kansas Hell." The whoop and war cry, the shout and Rebel Yell came from these aristocratic mixed bloods, dressed in patched Confederate gray, captured Yankee blue, as General Watie dressed, in baggy pants, with whatever coat available, and a mongrel military cloak when needed. The whoops and shouts sounded along the plains from the half wild brothers who restrained their impatience in the assaults on the Kansas Pins of another culture.

Snake Creek, IT

One last skirmish took place in Indian Territory on April 24, 1865, as three Confederate cavalrymen were blown out of their saddles in a hail of gunfire along Snake Creek in Choctaw Country. A Federal cavalry patrol out of Fort Gibson ran into a small detachment of Rebel troopers carrying mail north from Boggy Depot. The captured letters revealed these Confederates and their comrades did not know of Lee's surrender.

The fate of Indian Territory was decided when Lt. General Edmund Kirby-Smith surrendered the Trans-Mississippi Department on May 26, 1865. One by one, the Indian Rebels surrendered their forces. General Stand Watie, as Chief of the Cherokees held out, with his Southern flag still flying. He knew his subordinate commanders in Indian Territory had given up with dignity and with pride. Military leaders of the Indian Nations had halted operations as unconquered chieftains, relinquishing warfare against the hated abolitionists only because there was none left to fight along side them. Just as Stand Watie had planned!

Peter P. Pitchlynn, the chief of the Choctaw Nation surrendered the military forces of his tribe on June 19, and Winchester Colbert, governor of the Chickasaw Nation surrendered for his people and the Caddo. In a sense, the end of the Civil War in Indian Territory was anticlimactic, for the passions, surrounding the surrender of General Robert E. Lee at Appomattox on April 9 had subsided before the last surrender in Indian Territory. Confederate Chickasaw and Caddo Warriors made their surrender official on July 14, over three months after Appomattox.

Stand Watie, the proud and fiercely patriotic chief of the secessionist Cherokee, had the distinction of being the last Confederate officer of General rank to lay down his sword. On a hot, muggy June 23, 1865, General Stand Watie endured the hardest ride in his life. No Yankee guns aimed at him, no sabers slashing close to his body, no smell of gunpowder mixed with dust on a battlefield. He rode into Doaksville, a small community adjacent to Fort Towson in the Choctaw Nation, to sign a treaty of Cease Fire with the United States commissioners who had come for that purpose. When you read the treaty, notice it provides for a "CEASE FIRE" and the participants are to return to their homes.

THE CEASE FIRE TREATY.

Treaty stipulations made and entered into this 23rd day of June 1865 near Doaksville, Choctaw Nation, between Sent. Colonel A. C. Mathews and W. H. Vance U. S. V., commissioners appointed by Major General Herron U. S. A., on part of the military authorities of the United States and Brig. General Stand Watie, Governor and Principal Chief of that part of the Cherokee Nation lately allied with Confederate

States in acts of hostilities against the Government of the United States as follows to wit:

ARTICLE 1. All acts of hostilities on the part of both armies having ceased by virtue of a convention entered into on the 26th day of May 1865 between Major General E. R. S. Gantry U. S. A. Comdg. Trans. Miss. Department.

The Indians of the Cherokee Nation here represented, lately allied with the Confederate States in acts of hostilities against the Government of the United States, do agree at once to return to their respective homes and there remain at peace with United States, and offer no indignities, whatever, against the whites or Indians of the various tribes who have been friendly to or engaged in the service of the United States during the war.

ARTICLE II. It is stipulated by the undersigned commissioners on part of the United States, that so long as the Indians aforesaid observe the provisions of article first of this agreement, they shall be protected by the United States authorities in their person and property, not only from encroachment on the part of the whites, but also from the Indians who have been engaged in the service of the United States.

"ARTICLE III. The above articles of agreement to remain and be in force and effect until the meeting of the Grand Council to meet at Armstrong Academy, Choctaw Nation, on the 1st day of September, A. D. 1865, and until such time as the proceedings of said Grand Council shall be ratified by the proper authorities both of the Cherokee Nation and the United States. In testimony, whereof the said Lieut. Col. A. C. Mathews and Adjutant W. H. Vance, commissioners on part of the United States and Brig. General Stand Watie Governor and Principal Chief of the Cherokee Nation, have hereunto set their hands and seals.

Signed.

A. C. Mathews, Sent. Col.
W. H. Vance, Adjt.
Commissioners.
Stand Watie,
Brig. Genl. Governor and
Principal Chief Cherokee Nation,

The last Confederate officer to stop fighting, Brigadier General Stand Watie, with the full respect of his men and his enemies, turned his horse toward home. The ghostly Stars and Bars rippled across the hot June sky. The battles, shouts of Pins and Rebel Indians, screams of dying men and animals, Rebel Yells and the Stars and Bars on a Southern Charge, were now alive only in memories and the dust devils that swirled in the wind.

He had a bold dream, for his people and the South. The dreamer had strong courage and valor. Sometimes like a magician, he appeared, leaving devastation in his path, then he was gone. His troops like gray phantoms traveled the Indian country at will. He had been a strong force to contend with, a devil to find, and when found, you did not really want to be there. The dream was over, the dreamer awake.

This Cease Fire did not come with the pageantry that might have been expected from a guerilla fighter, who had captured the imaginations of both North and South. Confederate veterans and sympathetic writers kept Watie's legend alive. He became the example of devotion to the "Cause." Even enemy Cherokees came to respect his devotion to his beliefs, and "Stand" and "Watie" became common Cherokee first names.

Stand Watie's reputation was cemented at the Battle of Elkhorn Tavern/Pea Ridge. He captured a Union battery after a dramatic charge, and proved skillful in withdrawal helping to prevent a disaster. One of his soldiers said:

"I don't know how we did it, but Watie gave the order, which he always led, and his men would follow him into the jaws of death. The Indian Rebel Yell was given and we fought like tigers three to one. It must have been the mysterious power of Stand Watie that led us on to make the capture against such odds."

Watie stuck to the Southern cause. Untrained as a soldier, he had good sense and cunning and was an effective guerilla. Stand Watie and his men, with the Confederate Creeks, scoured the country at will. Watie was promoted to Brig. General on May 10, 1864. He had displayed unfailing courage, devotion, constant optimism, and good humor, at least according to his friends. He never, they say, had a harsh word for his family and never gave way to despair and dejection. In reality, he was not a shining cavalier - his Indian troops sometimes reverted to scalping and torture. He was clearly involved in some shameful political skullduggery. However, he was a man who fought hard for his beliefs and stuck to his guns even when the odds were against him. He supported two lost causes, the Ridges and then the Confederacy, but he had never given up.

After the war, Watie returned to absolute devastation. The Cherokee population before the war was 21,000 and had been reduced to 14,000. Homes had been destroyed, livestock decimated. There were no crops or seeds for them. The Nations were a war zone, in all that the phrase implies, leaving many widows and orphans. In his last years, his family dropped around him. All his sons died before he did on September 9, 1871, and his two young daughters followed in 1873.

The Cherokee in the Second and Third Kansas Home Guards played important roles in most battles in the Indian Nations as well as a few battles in Missouri and Arkansas. The deserters from Drew's Regiment received very little sympathy from Watie's Cherokees and many were killed when captured. After Drew's Regiment broke up in July 1862, Colonel John Drew continued his service in the Confederate Army as an officer. On August 25, 1865, Colonel Drew died a very poor and very sad man in a land ravaged by war.

After the war, the period of reconstruction in the Indian Nations was perhaps harder on the Indians than the people in the Southern states. Besides being defeated Confederates, they were still Indian, and suffered the prejudice associated with that, along with trying to rebuild their lives. The battles in their territory, raids by both sides, Jayhawkers, cattle thieves, had taken their stock; homes burned and must be rebuilt. They were Sovereign Nations, but no help was available to them.

Regardless of the outcome of the War Between the States, the Indians were the surest losers. Nations in the Territory, whether hostile or friendly to the United States during the war, were all punished by the appropriations of their land. In the Treaty of Washington in 1866, the United States required the sale of half the lands held by the Five Nations to make room for the tribes forced out of Kansas and Nebraska. Most of the Five Nations lands were taken by non-negotiable and unreasonable prices. Large numbers of the people were forced to move again for the second or third time in their lives. The government also seized two rights of ways for railroads through Indian Territory-----without compensation----to open routes for future white invasions into Indian lands.

The lands were not the only possession that would come under attack. After U. S. Grant became president in 1868, the "assimilation" of the Indian became official policy. In the end, the Civil War did not just cost the Indian his life and land; it also threatened his very identity as an Indian

Less than a year after the Cease Fire that was signed by General Watie, the Federal Cherokee delegates sold the old agency site of the Arkansas Cherokees: Transfer of 3400 acres of land, more or less. Situated in Township 7 Range 21, State of Arkansas. Said land being the former agency and residue of the tract disposed of by Cherokees by treaty of 1828. This effectively moved the Cherokee out of the state of Arkansas, at least on paper. Many Cherokee did not acknowledge this and stayed behind, since many of their ancestors had moved to the Missouri and Arkansas area before the end of the 1700's. The sale document states:

"Know all men by these presents, that whereas the Cherokee Nation owns a tract of land in the state of Arkansas, known as the Cherokee reservation lying in township No. 7, range 21, west of the Fifth Principal Meridian, and containing three thousand four hundred (3400) acres more or less, and all which is occupied or claimed by squatters and others claiming title adverse to the said Nation, under color of various titles. And whereas it is provided by the 4th Article of the treaty between the United States and the Cherokee Nation, of May 6th 1838, said tract shall be sold under the direction of the agent of the Cherokee Nation. And whereas the Cherokee Nation by its delegation hereto duly authorized, have sold said lands to John Brown Wright, of the city of Washington, and have received in payment therefore, the sum of five thousand dollars which they agree shall be applied by the Nation to the use named in said treaty and amendments thereto. Said sale having been made by direction and with the approval of Justin Harlin, the agent appointed by the United States for the Cherokee Nation. Now therefore, the said Cherokee Nation by its delegation hereto fully authorized to do, hereby request the Secretary of the Interior to cause a patent to be issued for the said John Brown Wright for the said land and do release the United States from all liability for said land or its proceed.

Witness our hands this, 10th day of May A. D. 1866.
          Daniel H. Ross
          White Catcher
          I. H. Benge
          James McDaniel
          Smith Christie
          B. Jones
          City of Washington, District of Columbia.

I, Justin Harlan agent of the United States for the Cherokee Nation, do hereby approve of and consent to the above sale, which was made by my direction this tenth day of May.

          J. Harlan, U. S. Indian Agent."

The United States Government knew the fighting between Cherokee factions in Indian Territory would certainly leave hard feelings and scars for many years to come. They needed to resettle Stand Watie's Southern Cherokees, their associated freed persons and former slaves and assure their civil rights and ability to govern themselves. Without looking to Ross Party Cherokees for justice and to avoid possible discrimination, this 1866 treaty established the Canadian district (and elsewhere if necessary) as their place of settlement. It also establishes seats or seats on the Cherokee National council for their representatives. The Dawes Commission enrollment procedures and lack of council representation after the turn of the century were injurious, unjust, and discriminatory towards Southern Cherokee. They were discouraged from settling in their rightful and promised lands in Indian Territory because of the defacto policies of the ruling Ross Party.

The Ross action leadership, later ratified by Congress - the Law of the Land, agreed to this treaty. One note, treaties *supersede* even the Constitution of the United States. The same signatures on this treaty are the ones who signed the previous document, selling the agency lands in Arkansas.

{July 19, 1866 | 14 Stat., 799 | Ratified July 27, 1866 | Proclaimed August 11, 1866}

Preamble

Treaty of February 18, 1863 between the Cherokees and the United States is declared void. A mutual amnesty is declared by both the Cherokee Nation and the United States, Confiscation laws are repealed, property sales which occurred under such laws are declared null and void, former ownership restored, purchasers repaid, etc.

The Canadian district established as a place of settlement for Southern Cherokees, freedmen and their former slaves.

~~~~~~~~~~~~

Articles of agreement and convention at the city of Washington, on the nineteenth day of July, in the year of our lord One Thousand Eight Hundred and Sixty-six, between the United States represented by Dennis N. Cooley, Commissioner of Indian Affairs, Elijah Sells superintendent of Indian Affairs for the southern superintendency, and the Cherokee Nation of Indian, represented by its delegates, James McDaniel, Smith Christie, White Catcher, S. H. Benge, J. B. Jones and Daniel H. Ross, principal chief of the Cherokees, being too unwell to join in these negotiation.

WHEREAS the existing treaties between the United States and the Cherokee Nation are deemed to be insufficient, the said contracting parties as follows, viz:

ARTICLE 1: The pretended treaties between the United States and the Cherokee Nation on the seventh day of October, eighteen hundred and sixty-one, and repudiated by the national council of the Cherokee Nation on the eighteenth of February, eighteen hundred and sixty-three is hereby declared to be void.

ARTICLE 2: Amnesty is hereby declared by the United States and the Cherokee Nation for all crimes and misdemeanors committed by one Cherokee on the person or property of another Cherokee or a citizen of the United States, prior to the fourth of July, eighteen hundred and sixty-six; and no right of action arising out of wrongs committed in aid or in the suppression of the rebellion shall be prosecuted or maintained in the courts of the United States or in the courts of the Cherokee Nation. But the Cherokee Nation stipulate and agree to deliver up to the United States, or their duly authorized agent, any or all public property, particularly ordnance stores, arms of all kinds, and quartermaster's stores, in their possession or control, which belonged to the so-called confederate States, without any reservation.

ARTICLE 3: The confiscation laws of the Cherokee Nation shall be repealed, and the same, and all sales of farms and improvements on real estate, made or pretended to be made in pursuance thereof, are hereby agreed and declared, to be null and void, and the former owners of such property, their heirs and assigns, shall have the right to peaceably reoccupy their homes and the purchaser under the confiscation laws, or his heirs and assigns, shall be repaid by the treasurer of the Cherokee Nation from the national funds, the money paid for such property and the cost of permanent improvements on such real estate, made thereon by since the confiscation sale; the cost of such improvements to be fixed by a commission , to be composed by one person assigned by the Secretary of the Interior and one by the principal chief of the Nation, which two may appoint a third in cases of disagreement, which cost so fixed shall be refunded to the national treasurer by the returning Cherokees within three years of the ratification thereof.

ARTICLE 4: All of the Cherokees and freed persons who were formerly slaves to any Cherokee and all free Negroes not having been such slaves, who resided in the Cherokee Nation, prior to June first, eighteen hundred and sixty-one, who may reside northeast of the Arkansas River and Southeast of the Grand River, shall have the right to settle in and occupy the Canadian district southwest of the Arkansas River, and also all of that tract of country lying northwest of Grand River, and bounded on the southeast by Grand River and west by the Creek reservation to the northeast corner thereof; from thence west on the north line of the creek reservation to the ninety-sixth degree of west longitude; thence north on said line of longitude so far that a line due east to Grand River will include a quality of land equal to one hundred and sixty acres for each person who may so elect to reside in the territory above -described in this article; Provided, that said part of said district north of the Arkansas River shall not be set apart until it shall be found the Canadian district is not sufficiently large to allow one hundred and sixty acres to each person desiring to obtain settlement under the provisions of this article.

ARTICLE 5: The inhabitants electing to reside in the district described in the preceding article shall have the right to elect all their local officers and judges, and the number of delegates to which their numbers may be entitled in any general council to be established in the Indian Territory under provisions of this treaty as stated in Article 12, and to control all their local affairs, and to establish all necessary police regulations and rules for the administration of justice in said district, not inconsistent with the constitution of the Cherokee Nation or the laws of the United States; Provided, the Cherokees residing in said district shall enjoy all the rights and privileges of other Cherokee who may elect to settle in said district under the provisions of this treaty; Provided also, That if any such police regulations or rules be adopted which in the opinion of the President, bear oppressively on any citizen of the nation, he may suspend the same. And all rules and regulations in said district, or in any other district of the nation, discriminating against citizens of other districts, are prohibited, and shall be void.

ARTICLE 6: The inhabitants of the said district hereinbefore described shall be entitled to representation according to numbers in the national council, and all laws of the Cherokee Nation shall be uniform throughout said nation. And should any law, either in its provisions or in the manner of its enforcement, in the opinion of the President of the United States, operate unjustly or injuriously in said district, he is hereby authorized and empowered to correct such evil, and to adopt the means necessary to secure the impartial administration of justice, as well as fair and equitable application and expenditure of national funds as between the people of this and every other district in said nation.

ARTICLE 7: The United States court to be created in the Indian Territory; and until such court is created therein, the United States district court, the nearest to the Cherokee Nation, shall have exclusive original jurisdiction of all causes, civil and criminal, wherein an inhabitant of the district hereinbefore described shall be a party, and where an inhabitant outside of said district, in the Cherokee nation, shall be he other party, as plaintiff or defendant in a civil case, or shall be defendant or prosecutor in a criminal case, and all process issued in said district by any officer of the Cherokee Nation, to be executed on an inhabitant residing outside of said district. And all process issued by any officer of the Cherokee Nation outside of said district, to be executed on an inhabitant residing in said district, shall be to all intents and purposes null and void, unless endorsed by the district judge for the district where such process is to be served, and said person, so arrested, shall be held in custody by the officer so arresting him, until he shall be delivered over to the United States marshal, or by consent to be tried by the Cherokee court; Provided, That any or all provisions of this treaty, which make any distinction in rights and remedies between the citizens of any district and the citizens of the rest of the nation, shall be abrogated whenever the President shall have ascertained, by an election duly ordered by him, that a majority of the voters of such district desire them to be abrogated, and he shall have declared such abrogation: And provided further that no law or regulation, to be hereafter enacted within said district thereof, prescribing a penalty for its violation, shall take effect or be enforced until ninety days from the date of its promulgation, either by publication in one or more newspapers of general circulation in said Cherokee Nation, or by posting up copies thereof in the Cherokee and English languages in each district where the same is to take effect, at the usual place of holding district courts.

ARTICLE 8: No license to trade in goods, wares, or merchandise shall be ranted by the United States to trade in the Cherokee Nation, unless approved by the Cherokee council except in the Canadian district, and such other district north of the Arkansas River and west of the Grand River occupied by the so-called Southern Cherokee, as provided in Article 4 of this treaty.

****

These articles pertain to Stand Watie's Southern Cherokee, showing them to be an "exception to the rule," and upholding their status as a separate government entity. Though Watie lobbied for a separate Nation for his Southern Cherokee, the government refused recognition and insisted on a single Nation.

Annie Abel defined the reconstruction period in Indian Territory as "political re-adjustment." The treaties of 1866 re-established relations between the Five Nations and the United States.

The United States government abandoned the Indians of Indian Territory in 1861 when it re-assigned troops to other areas and virtually invited the Confederacy to take over. After the Tribes had signed treaties with the Confederate Government, the United States failed to care for and help the Indian refugees that had fled to Kansas. Federal civilian and military officers joined in the theft of thousands of head of Indian owned livestock, magnifying the difficulty of post war economic recovery. U. S. Senator James Lane and Congressman S. C. Pomeroy, both from Kansas, pushed legislation in Congress to invalidate all previous treaties that defined and protected the land rights of the five tribes and authorize the removal of other Indian people from Kansas into Indian Territory. Iowa Senator James Harlan prepared legislation that would formally make Indian Territory a federal territory, complete with a governor and legislature, in effect denying the Nations Sovereignty status. Combined, these measures made up a massive campaign to strip the nations of Indian Territory of their political independence, their land, and natural resources. When coupled with the further requirements to free their slaves and admit Freedmen to full equality, reduced their citizens to poverty and dependence.

The negotiations of the 1866 Reconstruction Treaties, orchestrated by a trio of greedy anti-Indian legislators, former Iowa Senator, now Secretary of State, James Harlan, Commissioner Indian Affairs Dennis N. Cooley, and head of the Southern Superintendency, Eligah Sells, (also Iowans) reflected the principles of the Lane-Pomeroy legislation. The Harlan bill went beyond the grants of land for railroad construction through Indian lands. The negotiations rested on a single policy of expansion and development at the expense of the Indians. These treaties forced the Southern Nations to grant railroads rights of ways. This was the beginning of the land hungry whites to challenge Indian sovereignty.

Important sites, skirmishes and battles in
Indian Territory, 1861-1865

Armstrong Academy: Located Bryan County, 2.5 miles north of Bokchita on State Highway 22, then 2.5 miles east.

Served as a major Southern Administrative Center and troop assembly point throughout the Civil War. It was here that representatives of the Cherokee, Choctaw, Chickasaw, Creek, Seminole and Caddo formed the United Nations of Indian Territory. Armstrong Academy was re-named Chata Tamaha (Choctaw City) and designated the Capitol of the Choctaw nation.

Backbone Mountain: Located LeFlore County east of state Highway 112, 1 mile south of Pocola.

Sept. 1, 1863. The 3 hour battle fought on the mountain's summit. Confederate troops under Brig. Gen. William L. Cabell were defeated by Major Gen. James G. Blunt's Union Forces. The battle assured Federal control over Fort Smith and opened the Fort Towson - Fort smith Military Road.

Bayou Menard: Located south of U.S. Highway 62 where it crosses Bayou Menard in northeastern Muskogee County.

July 27, 1862. Major William A. Phillips' advance troops of the first Federal invasion of Indian Territory during the War Between the States encountered and routed a Confederate force.

Bloomfield Academy: Located Bryan County, 3 miles south of Achille and 1 mile northeast of Hendrix.

Frequent campsite of the Confederate Chickasaw Battalion during the War. The school opened as a seminary for Chickasaw girls in 1854, used for a hospital and commissary distribution. Extensive footings of the buildings, which burned in 1914, remain.

Boggy Depot: Atoka County, 11 miles west of Atoka, 6 miles east of Wapanucka on state Highway 7, then south 4 miles, now part a State Park.

Main Confederate Commissary Depot in Indian Territory during the War.

Strategically located at the intersection of the Texas Road and the military road between Fort Smith and Fort Arbuckle. The local Presbyterian Church served as a military hospital. 3 miles northeast of Boggy Depot a small skirmish took place on April 24, 1865, 15 days after Lee's surrender at Appomattox. 3 Confederate troopers were killed.

Buck Creek Camp: LeFlore County, 1 mile east of Bokoshe on State Highway 31, then .5 mile south, 2.25 miles east on county roads along the banks of Buck Creek.

Favorite campsite of the Confederate troops during the war. The First Choctaw and Chickasaw Regiment, CSA, was trained here.

Cabin Creek: Located Mayes County, 3 miles north of Pensacola on west bank of Cabin Creek.

July 1-2, 1863, first battle. Confederate Brig. Gen. Stand Watie attacked a Federal wagon train where the California Road crossed Cabin Creek. Col. James M. Williams, commanding the federal troops charged across the rain-

swollen creek, forced the Southerners to withdraw.
Allowed the Federals to re-supply and reinforce Fort Gibson, to maintain their hold on northern Indian Territory.

Cabin Creek: Located Mayes County, 3 miles north of Pensacola on west bank of Cabin Creek.
Sept. 18-19, 1864, second battle. Gen Watie, with Gen. Richard M. Gano's Texas troops, captured a Federal wagon train worth $1.5 million worth of supplies. Confederates destroyed the disabled wagons and injured mules, returned southward with 130 wagons of food clothing and ammunition. It was a major engagement of the War in the Territory.

Camp Armstrong: Bryan County 3 miles northeast of Bokchito.
1862-1865 Confederate Post used as hospital and rest camp.

Camp Brooken: Haskell County, northwest of the junction of State Highways 71 and 9, south bank of the Canadian River.
1862, Confederate campsite.

Camp Jumper: Pittsburg County, east side of U.S. Highway 69, 1.5 miles south of intersection with State Highway 113.
Established by the Confederacy during the as one of its outposts across IndianTerritory. It was named for Col. John Jumper, First Seminole Volunteer Cavalry.

Camp McCulloch: Cherokee County, near intersection of State Highway 82 and U.S. Highway 62.

1861, was staging area for the Confederate Campaign to drive O-pothle-yohola and the pro-Northern Indians out of Indian Territory at the beginning of the War.

Camp McIntosh: Caddo County, south side of the Washita River 25 miles north of State Highway 9 and 5 miles west of the Caddo-Grady County line.

Was westernmost of the 200 mile long Confederate outpost line maintained along the Canadian and Arkansas Rivers. Named for Col. James McQueen McIntosh (no relation to the Indian McIntosh brothers,) killed at the Battle of Pea Ridge.

Occupied intermittently during the War.

Camp Napoleon: Grady County, at Verden along State Highway 62.

May 26, 1865, meeting between representatives of the pro-Southern Cherokee, Choctaw, Creek, Seminole, Chickasaw, Caddo and Osage Indians and leaders of the Plains Kiowa, Arapaho, Cheyenne, Lipan, Caddo, Comanche, and Anadarko. More than 5,000 Indians attended the meeting, which produced a peace treaty between the Tribes at the close of the War.

Camp Pike: Haskell County, 1 mile northeast of the intersection of State Highways 9 and 2.

Frequent camping place for Confederate troops.

Camp Ross: Cherokee County, near Ross Cottage, John Ross' home at Park Hill.

Frequent camping site Confederate Troops.

Camp Steel: LeFlore County, just across the Arkansas-Oklahoma border from Fort Smith.

1862, Was Confederate Campsite during the winter.

Camp Wattles: Mayes County, near the mouth of Pryor Creek.
>July, 1862 Campsite used by both Confederate and Federal troops during the War. Established by Union Col. Robert W. Furnas, commander of First Indian Regiment during the first Federal Indian Expedition.
>Was a base of operations to help the pro-Northern Indians re-establishing control over the Northern part of Cherokee Nation. Shortly after Furnas and his pro-Northern Indian troops were forced to withdraw to Kansas.

Choska: Wagoner County, just east of where State Highway 104 crosses the Arkansas.
November 9, 1861.
>Campsite for Col. Douglas H. Cooper's troops after the Battle of Chusta-Talasah.

Chustenahlah: Osage County 4 miles west of Skiatook on State Highway 20 where it crosses Quapaw Creek, then 1 mile north, west side of the county road.
>December 26, 1861. Battle when Confederate Troops commanded by Col. James M. McIntosh intercepted more than 3,500 pro-Northern Creek and Seminole with Opothleyohola.

Chusto-Talasah (Caving Banks): Tulsa County, 5 miles south on U.S. Highway 75 from it's junction with State Highway 20, then 1 mile west and .5 mile south on county roads on the west side of the roadway at the horseshoe bend of Bird Creek.
>November 11, 1961, Battle between Opothleyohola's pro-Northern Creeks and

Seminoles and Confederate Col. Douglas H. Cooper's troops.

Concharty: Wagoner County, east of Stone Bluff on Concharty Creek, south of Arkansas River, northeast of US Highway 64.
> Campsite of Confederate Brig. General Douglas H. Cooper's supply wagon train during the battle of Round Mountain. After the battle, troops briefly camped at nearby Spring Hill to rest.

Coody's Bluff: Nowata County, south side of Verdigris River 4 miles from intersection US Highways 169 and 60 on county roads.
> Garrisoned by 500 Cherokee of Col. John Drew during early part of War.

Council Hill: Muskogee County, 2 miles east on US Highway 62 from Okmulgee-Muskogee County line, 4 miles south.
> Headquarters for pro-southern Creek units through the War.

Cowskin Prairie: Delaware County, west of State Highway 10 and north of State Highway 25 intersection.
> June 6, 1862, Site where Brig. General Stand Watie's troops were attacked by Federal force commanded by Col. Charles Doubleday.
> 1863, Pro-Northern Cherokee held National Council, adopted Cherokee Emancipation Proclamation, freeing slaves.

Creek Agency: Muskogee County, 1 mile west of US Highway 69 on Agency Hill.

October 15, 1863, skirmish between pro-Southern Creek and Cherokee and pro-Northern Cherokee and Osage.

Doaksville: Choctaw County, 1 mile North of Fort Towson on US Highway 70.
Confederate Capitol of Choctaw Nation 1860-1863, major War supply center.

Fort Arbuckle: Garvin County, 4.5 miles west on State Highway 7 from intersection with I-35 to Hoover, .25 mile north on county road.
May 3, 1861, two companies Federal Troops withdrew abandoned post.
May 5, Texas troops occupied.
Staging area for Confederate forces in Indian Territory.

Fort Arbuckle on the Arkansas: Tulsa County, north side of Arkansas River 2 miles north State Highway 151 from junction with State Highway 25, east on county road.
November 11, 1834, abandoned.
November 1861, some of O-pothle-yohola's pro-northern followers camped among the ruins before Battle of Round Mountain.

Fort Blunt: Muskogee County
August, 1863, surrounded Fort Gibson, built by Union General William A. Phillips to strengthen Gibson after Federals reoccupied by 6000 Federal Troops.

Fort Cobb: Caddo County, 1.5 miles east of town of Fort Cobb along east bluffs of Cobb Creek.
May, 1861, abandoned by Federal Troops, occupied by Col. William C. Young and Texas

State Troops. About 30 local Indians enlisted, Confederate service, served as guard for nearby Wichita Agency.
Abandoned August 1862.

Fort Coffee: LeFlore County, 4 miles north of Skullyville, built on Swallow Rock, overlooking Arkansas River.
    1838, Abandoned by Federal Troops, became Choctaw Boys Academy,
    1861- October 1863, occupied by Confederate troops till over run and burned by Federal troops.

Fort Davis (Cantonment Davis): Muskogee County, 1 mile north Bacone College, just east of where State Highway 16 crosses Arkansas River. South side of Arkansas River, 2 miles south of mouth of Verdigris River.
    November 1862, built by Confederates to Federal presence at Fort Gibson. Occupied intermittently until December 27, 1862, when Phillip's Federal Command captured and burned the buildings.

Fort Gibson: Muskogee County, in town of fort Gibson, east side of Grand River.
    September 1857, abandoned.
    1862, Reoccupied by Col. Phillip's Federals.

Fort McCulloch: Bryan county, .5 mile south of State Highway 22, 1.5 miles from junction with State Highway 48, 200 yards south of Blue River.
    March,1862, established by Confederate Brig. General Albert Pike after Battle of Pea Ridge, Arkansas.

July 21, 1862, Abandoned by Pike, later reoccupied by pro-Southern Troops.

Fort Towson (Cantonment Towson; Camp Phoenix):
Choctaw County, just north of US Highway 70 at Fort Towson.

May 1824, established as Cantonment Towson, abandoned 1829, buildings burned, re-established 1831 as Camp Phoenix due to Choctaw Removal, served as supply depot, and deactivated 1854.

1861, occupied by Confederate troops, as Fort Towson, served as regional Headquarters.

Fort Washita, Bryan County, north side State Highway 199, 3 miles west of junction with State Highway 18.

April 23, 1842, Established.

May 1, 1861 seized by Confederate forces, served as headquarters for Brig. General Douglas A. Cooper during War, major supply point and hospital facility.

Fort Wayne, (2nd site): Delaware County, 1.25 miles west of Oklahoma-Arkansas border, on State Highway 20 and 4.5 miles south on county roads.

1839, established to find healthier climate for troops at Old Fort Wayne (south of present site). Abandoned May 26, 1842.

July 1861, occupied by Brig. General Stand Watie, served as staging area for Cherokee Mounted Rifles, first unit raised for Confederacy in Indian Territory.

October 22, 1862 on nearby Beattie's Prairie, Brig. General James Blunt's Federal forces attacked Col. Douglas H. Cooper's Confederate

Indians. Gave Federal Army command of Indian Territory north of Arkansas River.

George Washington Caddo's Home: Canadian County, south side of North Fork of Canadian River, 5 miles west of Union City.

1864, George Washington Caddo commissioned a major in Confederate Army, authorized to raise Caddo Battalion to prevent raids by Plains Indians into areas occupied by Five Civilized Tribes.

Goodland Mission: Choctaw County, 1.5 miles east on State Highway 2A from junction with US Highway 271.

Mobilization site for two companies of Second Choctaw Regiment, CSA, during War.

Greenleaf Town: Okfuskee County, 3 miles west of Okemah on state Highway 56 from junction with State Highway 27, 1 mile south on county road.

August 1861, gathering site for O-pothle-yohola's followers. Old town site was probably west of the road along the creek.

November 1861, O-pothle-yohola led the Loyal Indians north toward Kansas.

Harris Ferry: McCurtain County, below Harris OK, where State Highway 87 nears Red River.

Major communications point Indian Territory Confederates and Texas troops during War.

Honey Springs: McIntosh and Muskogee Counties, along Elk Creek on east and west sides US Highway 69 for 1 mile north and one mile south of county line.

July 17, 1863, Major General James G. Blunt's 3,000 Federal troops assaulted 5,000

Confederate troops deployed along Elk Creek. Confederates, with wet powder that would not fire, were forced out. Broke the power of the Confederacy in Indian Territory for remainder of War.

Iron Bridge: Haskell County, 1.25 miles south of where State Highway 9 crosses San Bois Creek.
> June 16 and 19, 1864, skirmish following Brig. General Stand Watie's capture of J. R. Williams. Bridge built in 1859 by Federal government as part of Butterfield Stage route. Frequently used by Federal and Confederate troops during War.

Pleasant Bluff: Haskell County, northeast edge of Tamaha along Arkansas.
> June 15, 1864, Brig. General Stand Watie ambushed and captured Federal supply steamboat J. R. Williams, hauling supplies from Fort Smith to Fort Gibson. Disabled with cannon fire from bluffs overlooking river, drove it to shore, forced Federal escort to abandon, captured $120,000.00 worth of supplies.

Koweta Mission: Wagoner County, 2.5 miles east on county road from intersection State Highway 52 and Muskogee Turnpike.
> July 1861, seized by Confederates.
> July 1862, Re-occupied by Federal troops.

Locust Grove: Mayes County, south of US Highway 412, 2.5 miles east of Locust Grove.
> July 3, 1862, skirmish, 300 Federals under Col. William Weer surprised Confederate Col. J. J. Clarkson's camp, forcing Clarkson and 110 men to surrender.

Middle Boggy: Atoka County, 1 mile north of Atoka, on North side of Middle (Muddy Boggy) Creek.

> Frequent campsite for Southern troops during War. Local cemetery contains Confederate graves.
>
> February 14, 1864, some elements of Col. John Jumper's Seminole Battalion, Captain Adam Nail's 1st Choctaw and Chickasaw Cavalry and 20th Texas Cavalry were surprised and defeated by Union force of part of 14th Kansas Cavalry and artillery.

New Springplace: Cherokee county, 1.5 miles southeast of Oaks.

> Site of Moravian Mission, established 1842. Mission buildings burned by pro-northern Cherokee during War.

Park Hill: Cherokee County Intersection State Highway 82 and Us Highway 62.

> Site of Rose Cottage, Principle Chief John Ross' home. Brig. General Stand Watie burned to ground during War.

Perryville: Pittsburg County, intersection of US Highway 69 and Indian Nations Turnpike.

> Major Confederate Military establishment and supply point during War.
>
> August 25, 1863, Major General James K. Blunt's Federal forces routed elements of Brig. General William F. Steel's Confederate forces, seized the town and burned the supplies and buildings.

Pleasant Grove Mission; Johnston County. .75 mile west of Emet

Col. William H. Emory concentrated Federal troops from Forts Washita and Arbuckle in this area at beginning of War.

May 2, 1861, 2nd Lt. William W. Averell made contact with Emory's column 1.5 miles south junction State Highways 99 and 7 with dispatch from Washington D.C. ordering Emory to withdraw all Federal troops to Kansas.

Pryor Creek: Mayes County, 3.5 miles south of Adair along both sides US Highway 69.

Battle took place after Confederate victory at Second Cabin Creek commanded by Col James M. Williams.

Round Mountain: Pawnee County, on edge of Lake Keystone, 3.5 miles north on State Highway 48, from where it crosses Pawnee-Creek Counties line.

November 19, 1861, Col. Douglas H. Cooper's Confederate troops caught pro-northern Creek and Seminole under O-pothle-yohola fleeing to Kansas.

San Bois Creek: Haskell County, along south side of State Highway 9 where it crosses San Bois Creek.

August 30, 1863, Confederate force encountered advance guard of Major General James K. Blunt's Federals advancing on Skullyville. Running fight followed along 10 miles of road east of San Bois Creek.

Sell's Store: Creek County, 3.25 miles east of Slick where State Highway 16 crosses Brown's Creek.

Fall, 1861, served as Col. Douglas H. Cooper's headquarters, during search for O-pothle-yohola's Creeks as they fled to Kansas.

Seminole Council House: Pottawatomie County, 3 miles east of Tribbey on county road.
>August 1, 1861, treaty signed between Confederate Brig. General Albert Pike and Principal Chief John Jumper of Seminole

Skullyville: LeFlore County, along both sides State Highway 9, between Spiro and Skullyville.
>August 31, 1863, Skirmish took place along Fort Towson-Fort Smith Military road, between elements of Major General James K. Blunt's Union force and Brig. General William A. Cabell's Confederate force.

Tahlequah: Cherokee County, junction State Highway 51 and US Highway 62, capitol of Cherokee Nation.
>July 1861, Brig. General Stand Watie raised Confederate Flag above the square and declared his intention to fight for the South.

Thioplocco Town: Okfuskee County, 7 miles south, 1 mile east of Okemah on State Highway 27.
>October, 1861, skirmish between pro-Southern and pro-Northern Creek.
>October 1861, Confederate Col. Douglas H. Cooper at the community while chasing O-pothle-yohola's Loyal Indians north to Kansas.

Tullahassee Mission: Wagoner county, 1.5 miles west on State Highway 51B from junction with US Highway 69, then .5 mile north on county road.
>July 1861 occupied by Confederate forces, buildings used for hospitals, barracks, stables.

Tulsey Town: Tulsa County, along banks of Arkansas River, 2.5 miles north of I-44 bridge over the Arkansas in present day Tulsa.
    Well known Creek settlement. Confederate Col. Douglas H. Cooper left his supply train there while his men pursued O-pothle-yohola's followers after Battle of Chustenahlah.

Wapanucka Academy: Johnston County, 2.25 miles north of junction State Highways 7 and 7D, then 1.25 miles east.
    Used as Confederate military hospital and prison during War.

Washita River: Garvin County, along State Highway 193 miles southwest of junction with State Highway 133.
    First Civil War encounter in Indian Territory. Col. William H. Emory's withdrawing column of Federal troops captured vanguard of Col. William C. Young's Texas troops, pursuing Texas Troops. After agreeing to discontinue their pursuit, Texas troops were released and followed at discreet distance behind Federals.

Webber's Falls: Muskogee County, where US Highway 64 crosses Arkansas River.
    April 11, September 9, October 12, 1863. Minor skirmishes, Confederate and Union.
    April 25, 1863, Col. William A. Phillips' Federal troops' surprised meeting of Confederate Cherokee National Council scheduled to convene in Webber's Falls, capturing their supplies and dispersing the delegates.

Wheelock Mission: McCurtain County, 2 miles east of Millerton.

Quarters and staging area for Confederates several occasions during War.

Wichita Agency: 3 miles north of Anadarko on US 281 from junction with US highway 62, then 5 miles west on county road.

Established 1859 as first Federal Indian Agency in western Indian Territory.

August 12, 1861, Site where Confederate Commissioner Albert Pike negotiated treaties with 11 tribes, resulting in 2 treaties.

October 23, 1863, federally armed force of Delaware, Shawnee, Osage, Seminole, Cherokee destroyed the agency, and massacred pro-Southern Tonkawa camped nearby.

Indian Territory Maps

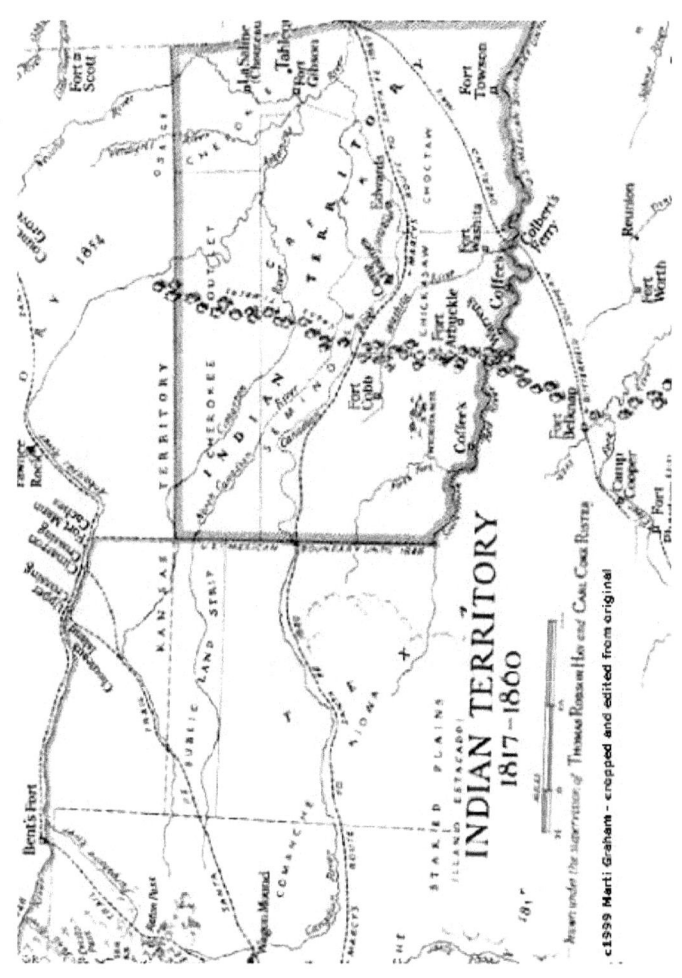

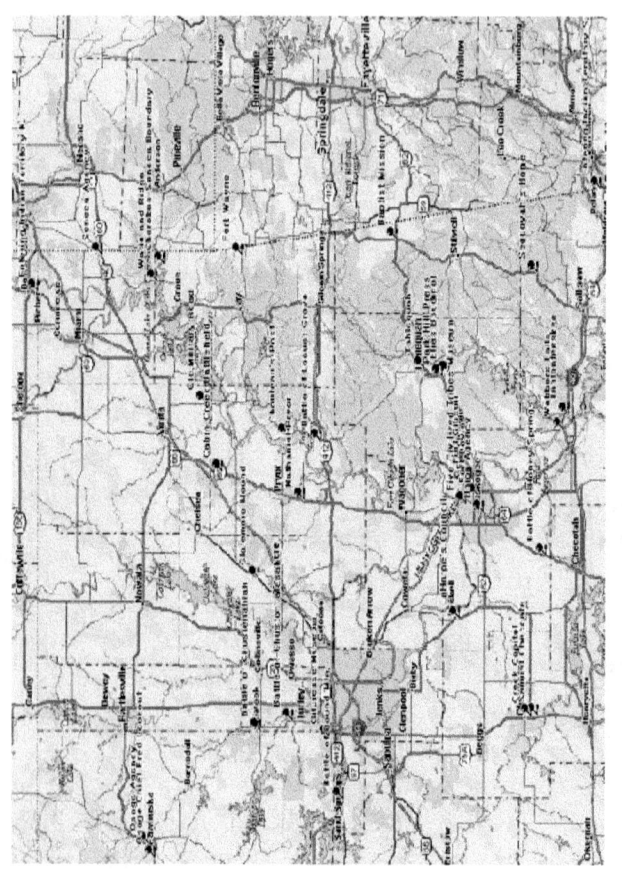

RESOURCES

The American Indian and the End of the Confederacy 1863-1866 by Annie Heloise Abel, Theda Perdue University of Nebraska Press, Lincoln and London, Bison Book Reprint, 1993

Civil War in the Indian Territory by Steve Cottrell, Pelican Publishing Co., Gretna, LA, 1998

BETWEEN TWO FIRES: American Indians in the Civil War
by Laurence Hauptman The Free Press 1995

Now the Wolf Has Come: The Creek Nation in the Civil War
by Christine Schultz White and Benton R. White, Texas A. & M. Press, 1996

General Stand Watie's Confederate Indians: Confederate Indians by Frank Cunningham, Brad Agnew

The American Indian in the Civil War, 1862-1865 by Annie Heloise Abel, University of Nebraska Press, Lincoln and London, Bison Book Reprint, 1993

Sam Bell Maxey and the Confederate Indians (Civil War Campaigns and Commanders) by John C. Waugh

The American Indian As Slaveholder and Secessionist by Annie Heloise Abel, University of Nebraska Press, Lincoln and London, Bison Book Reprint, 1993

Red Fox: Stand Watie and the Confederate Indian Nations During the Civil War Years in Indian Territory by Wilfred Knight Arthur C. Clark Co. 1988

Opothleyaholo and the Loyal Muskogee: Their Flight to Kansas in the Civil War by Lela J. McBride Brockway Tindle

The Confederate Cherokees: John Drew's Regiment of Mounted Rifles by W. Craig Gaines

Slaveholding Indians: The American Indian As Participant in the Civil War 1919 by Annie H. Abel University of Nebraska Press, Lincoln and London, Bison Book Reprint, 1993

Civil War in the Indian Territory by Lary C. Rampp

Oklahoma: A History of the Sooner State.
by Edwin C. Reynolds, University of Oklahoma Press, 1954, 1964

History of the Cherokee...by Emmett Starr, 1921

A Creek Warrior for the Confederacy: The Autobiography of Chief G. W. Grayson...Edited by W. David Baird, University of Oklahoma Press, 1988

Confederate Cavalry West of the River...Stephen B. Oates, Austin, University of Texas Press, 1961

The Civil War Rea in Indian Territory...Edited by LeRoy H. Fischer, Lorrin L. Morrison, Pub. 1974

General Jo Shelby - Undefeated Rebel....Daniel O'Flareharty

The Union Indian Brigade in the Civil War.....Wiley Britton, Franklin Hudson Publishing Company, Kansas City, Missouri, 1922

<u>Compiled Service Records Of Confederate Soldiers From the Indian Territory</u> contains the list of Microfilm rolls/numbers for each unit.

Web Sites
<u>A Guide to Cherokee Confederates</u> Thomas's Legion Civil War Cherokees in North Carolina

<u>Warriors and Chiefs</u> Stand Watie: Cherokee Chief and Confederate General
<u>Warriors in the Union</u>
<u>Brig. General Stand Watie</u>
<u>John Ross</u> Leader of the Cherokee
<u>Fort Washita Civil War Reports</u>

OFFICIAL RECORDS: Series 4, vol 34, Part 2, page 950

OFFICIAL RECORDS: Vol. 22, Part 1, page 380

OFFICIAL RECORDS: Vol. 41, Part 3, page 300

OFFICIAL RECORDS: Vol. 41, Part 2, page 1082

OFFICIAL RECORDS: Vol. 41, Part 1, pages 780-782; 785-786; 787-788; 791; 771-772; 766-771; 767-768; 790-792;

Department of Interior Files, Letters

Department of Interior, Office of Indian Affairs, 1862-1866, General Files

Office of Indian Affairs, Southern Superintendency, 1863-1864

Commissioner of Indian Affairs, Reports, 1862-1865

General Orders No. 11, US Army

<u>Interview With Doug Keller</u> by Michael A. Hughes, Journal Of the Indian Wars, Vol. 1, No. 3, Savas Publishing Co., 2000

<u>Flowing with Blood and Whiskey</u>: Stand Watie and the Battles of First and Second Cabin Creek, by Palmer Boeger, Journal of The Indian Wars, Vol. 1, No. 3, Savas Publishing Co., 2000

<u>African Creek Soldiers Enter the Civil War,</u> by Gary Zeller, Journal Of the Indian Wars, Vol. 1, No. 4, Savas Publishing Co, 2000

www.ingramcontent.com/pod-product-compliance
Lightning Source LLC
Chambersburg PA
CBHW071939160426
43198CB00011B/1463